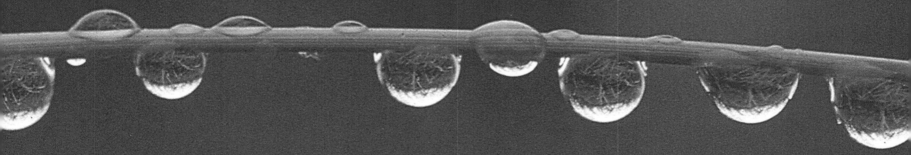

THE KIMCHEE COOKBOOK

The Kimchee Cookbook
The Fiery Flavors and Cultural History of Korea's National Dish

Published by Periplus Editions Ltd
Copyright © 1999 Periplus Editions Ltd
First published by Design House Publishers, Inc, 1997

Publisher: Eric Oey
Editor: Kim Inglis
Food Editor: Foong Ling Kong
Designer: Loretta Reilly Chan

ISBN 962-593-506-1

Distributed by:
Berkeley Books Private Limited
5 Little Road, #08-01
Singapore 536983
Tel: 65.280 1330

Tuttle Publishing (USA)
364 Innovation Drive
North Clarendon
VT 05759-9436
Toll-free order number: 1-800-526-2778

Tuttle Publishing (Japan)
RK Building, 2nd Floor
2-13-10 Shimo-Meguro
Meguro-ku
Tokyo 1530064
Tel: 81-3-5437-0171

the kimchee cookbook

FIERY FLAVORS AND CULTURAL HISTORY OF KOREA'S NATIONAL DISH

BY KIM MAN-JO, LEE KYOU-TAE, LEE O-YOUNG

PERIPLUS

CONTENTS

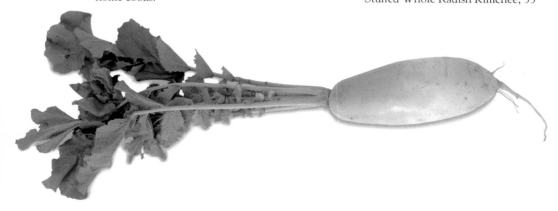

THE ORIGINS, HISTORY AND CULTURE OF KIMCHEE

From ancient times to the present day, the fiery flavors of
kimchee have dominated the Korean cultural landscape.
Here we trace the development of the various types of
kimchee, its references in Korean literature, past and
present, and place it in its historical context. Both
as a symbol of Korean cosmology and as an ordinary
item in every household, kimchee is a unique
dish found nowhere else in the world.

It is generally acknwledged in the West that there are four cardinal tastes: sweet, sour, bitter, and salty. Koreans, however, have an additional one, which they regard above those, namely, pungency. Pungency is one of the indispensable tastes in every Korean meal, necessary for stimulating the flow of saliva and the appetite.

The unique pungency of Korean food is the fermented flavor that is found in pickles (kimchee) and basic Korean condiments such as soybean sauce, soybean paste and chili paste. This flavor is the result of a kind of 'controlled spoilage' and is a distinctive characteristic of Korean cuisine.

Preserving Food

Drying was the very first method humans used to preserve foods. Later, they discovered that foods could also be preserved by salting, and later still, by fermentation. Although it was possible to store grains and nuts for long periods without using any of these methods, foods with high moisture content such as fish, meats, and vegetables could not be kept for any reasonable length of time without some special method of preservation. With vegetables, drying was not only difficult to carry out successfully, but also caused the vegetables to lose their nutritional value and flavor. Once salt was discovered, it was found that foodstuffs stored in salt both kept well and were good to eat. Salting softened fibers, making the vegetables easier to chew, and induced amino and lactic acid fermentation. The earliest salt was found in seawater, rock-salt deposits or salt flats. Later, commercial salt was used.

Since ancient times, Korean people preserved wild vegetables by pickling. They also developed and mastered the techniques of salting, brining and fermenting. Once cultivation of vegetables began and herbs and spices were introduced from abroad, these new ingredients were mixed with existing ones to create new forms of foods. Such newly introduced vegetables were adapted to the Korean land and climate, and further developed.

The development of the kinds of kimchee Koreans eat today started when vegetables were brought in from abroad; especially revolutionary was the introduction of cabbages that formed a dense head. New concoctions made use of wild vegetables to create new kinds of kimchees, such as the *honhap kimchee*, *sokpakchi*, and *pyolmi kimchee*. The cultivation of head cabbages also led to the development of lactic-acid fermentation. As people experienced the efficacy of using spices and fermented fish paste in addition to fish or meat as appropriate, the kinds of kimchees commonly found today gradually came into being.

Defining Kimchee

The earliest record of kimchee is in China's oldest collection of poetry, the *Book of Odes*, which was written nearly 3,000 years ago. The section entitled 'Xiao Ya' contains a stanza: "On the bank of the field, a cucumber has grown. If you slice it up, pickle it, and offer it to your ancestors, your progeny will live long and you'll receive the blessings of Heaven." The character for pickle (pronounced *ju* in Chinese and *cho* in Korean) means kimchee. This *ju* is the ancestor of kimchee.

The earliest appearance of this character in extant Korean literature occurs in *Tonggugisanggukship* or the *History of the Koryo Dynasty*, written by Yi Kyu-bo (1168–1241). Nevertheless, it would be unreasonable to assume that this is actually the oldest documented reference to kimchee in Korea. Some scholars believe the word kimchee is derived from a combination of two Chinese characters meaning 'salted vegetables.' In August 1966, at the Second International Academic Conference on Food Science and Engineering in Warsaw, Poland, it was decided that k-i-m-c-h-e-e should be the official English spelling of this Korean national dish.

Above: Rice is always served in Korean households along with vegetable, meat or fish dishes and the ubiquitous kimchee.

Far left: This ceramic jar, from the Kaya Confederation (c. 1st century AD), measures 89 cm in height, 55 cm across the mouth, 117 cm around the neck and 227 cm around the belly. Made of baked clay, it was used to store or move foodstuffs. The big clay jars commonly unearthed at sites that date to the period of the Three Kingdoms often show signs of having been used to store kimchee.

Above left: The character for pickle – pronounced *ju* in Chinese and *cho* in Korean.

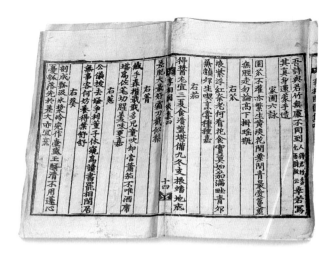

History

The earliest written references to kimchee date from the second half of the Koryo Dynasty (918–1392). Nevertheless, in view of the fact that such Chinese texts as the *Hou Zhou Shu* say that cereals, fruits, and vegetables were grown in Paekche and Silla as they were in China, and the production of alcoholic beverages was the same as in China, it seems quite likely that kimchee-like fermented vegetable dishes were already being made and eaten during Korea's Three Kingdom period (4th century–mid-7th century). This was an era when exchanges with China flourished. Methods of pickling vegetables would have been similar to those used in China, and because this period predates the cultivation of vegetables brought in from distant lands, it is probable that the vegetables used in kimchee were local wild species.

Korean food underwent great changes during the Choson Dynasty (1392–1894). Of paramount importance was the introduction of chilies at the end of the 16th century. Some scholars maintain that chilies were brought to Korea directly by Portuguese soldiers who were among the Ming reinforcements that aided Korea during the Japanese invasions. (Whether this is true or not, it is known that chili powder was not widely used in kimchee until the 18th century, nearly 200 years after chili peppers were introduced.) Korean people have always had a taste for food that is hot, both in terms of temperature and spiciness, and the strong flavors of mustard and black pepper have always been popular. When chilies became available, Koreans started to add them to kimchee, which had previously been pickled in a brine flavored with Japanese pepper or fennel. They learned that chilies helped to keep kimchee from spoiling and allowed for the use of less salt.

Opposite, far left: A painting by an anonymous artist of the Choson Dynasty. The earliest extant record of cabbage in Korea is found in a Koryo Dynasty book entitled *Hyangyakkugumbang*, but references to cabbage in books on agriculture were rare until the middle of the Choson Dynasty. Before this, radish was the main vegetable. It was not common to make kimchee out of cabbage until the introduction of *Brassica pekinensis* from China some time after it was first cultivated in the region of Beijing in the mid 1700s.

Opposite, left: *Tonggugisanggukchip (History of the Koryo Dynasty)*, written by Yi Kyu-bo of the Koryo Dynasty, is believed to contain the oldest extant written reference to kimchee in Korea. The book is open at the section entitled 'Kapoyugyong,' a poem about six vegetables grown in home gardens: cucumbers, eggplant, turnips, Welsh onions and gourds.

Far left: Old map of Korea.

Left: The origin of Japanese pickled radish is *chogangji* (*ji* meaning pickle), but the etymology and meaning of *chogang* are not clear. In the *Kojiki*, an 8th-century Japanese history book, there is the story of a man named Chogang who crossed over from Kudara (the Japanese name for Paekche) during the reign of the emperor Ojin and taught the local people how to brew with malt. Perhaps this indicates that *chogangji* was introduced to Japan from ancient China via Paekche.

Above: A vegetable market of the Choson Dynasty, with piles of long skinny cabbages on display.

Above: Examples of a stone and a wooden mortar. Big mortars were used for pounding barley and other grains, but the smaller ones served to grind up such seasonings as garlic, sesame seeds and ginger. Sometimes large natural rocks were placed in the courtyard near the well and hollowed out to be used as mortars for crushing or grinding chilies. When the hollow became worn very deep after long use, it was put to use as the mortar for a much larger pestle attached to a treadle.

Kimchee Through the Years

Throughout Korean history, there are a number of written references to the use of kimchee, the types being produced at certain times and the methods employed. Not only do these shed light on the cultural context in which kimchee is eaten, they help to trace the development of processes and the periods various ingredients were introduced. Below are listed some of the major references:

A kimchee called *paktimch'ai* is mentioned in *Kani Pyogonbang* (*The Easy Way To Drive Out Epidemics*), published in the 20th year of the reign of King Chungjong of Choson (1525). The passage says that adults and children alike should drink the liquid of *nabak* kimchee made from turnips. This is the first written reference to *nabak* kimchee (a watery kimchee).

Another book dating from the mid-Choson Dynasty that refers to pickled vegetables is *Chubangmun*. It describes *yakchihi*, a medicinal pickle made of eggplant, cucumbers and bamboo shoots seasoned with black pepper, garlic, and green onions (the mixture is fried and then immersed in boiled soy sauce); *saenggangch'im* (ginger pickled in vinegar); *t'imgosari* (salted bracken); a kind of *ch'imch'ae* made with cucumbers, eggplant and radish pickled in a hot brine; and *ch'ongt'aech'im*, made of *ch'ongt'ae* beans preserved in salt. (Chilies are not mentioned, indicating that they were not yet being used.)

Umsik Timibang, a cookbook written in Hangul in about 1670 by a woman of the Andong Chang clan, contains recipes for a kimchee made of wax gourd pickled in salt, and one made by pouring warm water over wild Indian mustard leaves in a jar which was placed on a heated floor to ferment the mixture. This method is called *muyom ch'imch'ae*, or 'saltless fermentation.' It also includes more exotic recipes that use pickled pheasant flesh and pheasant meat, but the most popular was the *nabak* kimchee, an everyday kimchee that would have been served in many Korean households.

Far left: Two Choson Dynasty women, most likely the lady of the house and her daughter-in-law, pound chilies in a mortar. Mortars and pestles were essential implements in farming households, where they were used to grind grains, pound steamed rice into cake dough, pulverize soy beans and so on.

The pestle was thinner in the middle to make it easier to handle, yet the work was very hard physically and the technique for wielding the pestle properly had to be acquired through practice. A hollowed-out section of a log used as a mortar was a common sight at farmsteads around the Korean countryside until not so long ago.

Above left: Metal mortars and pestles for grinding seasonings.

Above: *Umsik Timibang*, by Lady Sokkye (1598–1680) of the Andong Chang clan, was the first cookbook written in Hangul. It includes recipes for wild Indian mustard leaf kimchee, pheasant meat kimchee and other kinds of pickled pheasant flesh, and *nabak* kimchee (a watery kimchee made with flat slices of radish).

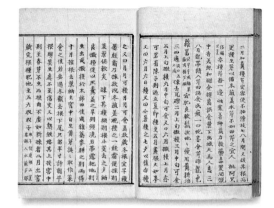

Above: Jars used for storing such seasonings as sesame salt, chili powder, and soy sauce.

Above right: *Chungo Sallim Kyongje (The Expanded Countryside Economy)* (c. 1766) contains the first mention of the use of chilies and chili powder in kimchee. Many of the types of kimchee mentioned are similar to those of today, indicating that contemporary types of kimchee began to establish themselves in the mid-18th century.

The recipe for *saengch'i ch'imch'ae* calls for cucumbers that have been peeled and julienned to be soaked in cold water. Boiled pheasant meat is sliced up like the cucumber, and both ingredients are combined in a warm brine to ferment like *nabak* kimchee. There are also recipes for kimchees that combine vegetables and fish or meat. Among them are *saengch'i tchanjihi* and *saengch'ichihi*, which use pickled cucumber fried in oil with pheasant meat and a seasoning of soy sauce.

In 1655 a man named Sin Sok compiled a book entitled *Nongga Chipsong (A Compendium for the Farming Household)*. It contains an almanac-like section listing dishes eaten during the various seasons of the year. Two of the foods recorded here are *ch'imgwajo* and *ch'imjupcho*. The latter is made by mixing eggplant, berries and wheat bran and burying the concoction in hot horse manure for about a month. This corresponds to today's *kanjangji*.

Eleven different kinds of kimchee are described in the book *Yorok (Important Records)*, dating from the late 1600s. None of them list chili peppers as an ingredient. Only kimchees made of radish, cabbage, wax gourd, bracken, *ch'ongt'ae* beans and other such vegetables are given, along with an explanation of *tongch'imi*, a watery dish made by salting radishes whole. The *muyom ch'imch'ae*, or 'saltless kimchee' described is made by immersing radish in clear water and leaving it for three to four days until a froth develops, at which point the liquid is drained off, fresh water added, and the radish allowed to ferment further.

Around 1715, Hong Man-Son wrote a book entitled *Sallim Kyongje (Counstryside Economy)*; it had a section on cookery that contained descriptions of various types of kimchee. Most of them do not contain chilies but are made by pickling vegetables in salt or vinegar, in some cases with spices.

Left and below: Implements used for grinding spices. Left is a *maja*, used by inserting the fingers in the holes and scraping at the seasonings with the rough, rounded surface. Below, a glazed ceramic bowl with a rough interior texture.

The book introduces five kinds of kimchee called *cha*, a variant of *cho*. These *cha*-type kimchees consist of rice and salted and fermented fish, making them similar to the fish *sikhae* dishes of today.

Sallim Kyongje divides kimchee production into two categories: those that employ bland methods requiring only small amounts of salt and those that use salty methods. (The author puts cabbage kimchee in the bland category.) He also divides cucumber kimchees into two groups: the *tchanji* type, simply preserved in salt, and the *sobagi* type, in which the cucumbers are stuffed with spices and herbs. Other kimchees described in the book are *Yongin oiji* (a cucumber pickle), winter eggplant kimchee, abalone kimchee and oyster kimchee.

Chungbo Sallim Kyongje (*The Expanded Country-side Economy*), published in about 1766 at the end of the reign of King Yongjo (r. 1724–76), was written by Confucian scholar Yu Chung-Im and is an expanded version of the earlier book. It does not have a separate section on kimchee, but in the gardening chapter the author names some vegetables and mentions *cho* (kimchee) as a common way of processing them and chili powder as an ingredient in some kimchees.

The description of radish *tchanji* says that it is made of radishes with their stems and leafy tops still attached, sea staghorn, pumpkin and eggplant; spiced with chilies, Japanese pepper and mustard; and immersed in garlic juice. It is similar to today's *chonggak* kimchee. He describes a yellow cucumber kimchee as being made by cutting three slits in each cucumber, stuffing the slits with chili powder and garlic and allowing the kimchee to

Above: In the forested, mountainous region of Kangwon Province, wooden crocks were developed. A section of log was hollowed out and fixed to a base. Such wooden crocks offered the advantages of easy portability and long-lasting durability. They were widely used instead of the more fragile ceramic variety. The one shown here is the largest extant wooden crock in Korea, measuring 128 cm in height and having a diameter of 80 cm. The diameter of the base is 152 cm.

Above right: In olden times when one bought pickled shrimp paste (*saeu chot*) it came in a small crock like this. When the shrimp boats caught great quantities of shrimp at a time, they pickled them in crocks right there on board to keep them from spoiling before they could get them to market.

Since pot-bellied crocks took up too much space compared to their storage capacity, crocks shaped for more compact storage were developed. It is surmised that the circumference of the bottom was made smaller than that of the mouth so that the hands could be inserted between the crocks more easily for moving them around. Similar crocks were used for other kinds of *chotkal*.

ferment, a dish that resembles today's *oi sobagi*. This book documents the use of chilies and chili powder, and also of garlic, green onions and chives as kimchee seasonings rather than main ingredients, a further step in the development of the use of chili in kimchee.

During this period Korean kimchee also spread to China. In Kim Chang-Op's 1712 account of his travels in that country, he says: "There was an old woman there who had immigrated from Korea and made her living by making kimchee. Her *tongchimi* tasted exactly like that made in Seoul." In *Kyesangijong*, published in 1803, the author writes: "The kimchee at the interpreter's house was made in imitation of our own and was quite good." Although we cannot be sure exactly what sort of kimchee this was, the reference provides one more piece of evidence that Korean kimchee had spread to China and gained popularity there. What is known, however, is the contemporary Chinese kimchee called Sichuan *paocai* that resembles Korean *tongchimi*. It seems that *tongchimi* was introduced to Sichuan by some of the Sichuanese soldiers sent to Korea to help fight off the Hideyoshi invasions during the Ming Dynasty.

During the 18th and 19th centuries, there are more and more written references to kimchee: *Kyongdo Chapchi* by Yu Tuk-Tae (1747–1800) gives a recipe for making *sokpakchi*: "Boil a broth of fermented baby shrimp paste and allow it to cool. Add radish, cabbage, garlic, chili pepper, turban shell flesh (*Turbo cornutus*), abalone and croaker. Store." The author says the concoction ferments to a spicy-hot flavor. Another interesting title, *Imwon Simnyukchi*, written by So Yu-Gu in 1872, presents a complete compendium of 19th-century Korean cookery. It divides the various kimchees into four types: *omjangchae*, *chachae*, *chechae* and *chochae*. *Omjangchae* includes kimchees that are usually eaten in the winter months; they are fermented in salt, brewing dregs and spices and are intended to be stored for long periods of time. *Chachae* and *chochae* are some-

Left and above: The design and special characteristics of crocks for storing kimchee vary from region to region. In such regions as Pyongan Province and Hamgyong Province, where the winters are long and cold, kimchee crocks are very large but shorter and fatter than those of the south. Those of the Hoeryong district of Hamgyong Province are known for their peculiar blueish-black color from lye added to the black glaze.

The crocks of the southern regions are generally smaller. Those of the central part of the country (Kyonggi and Chungchong provinces) are tall and slender. In Kyongsang Province (the south-eastern part of the peninsula) the crocks are small and of coarse design. The crocks of southern Chungchong Province have a pleasing oval shape and a narrow mouth, while those of the Cholla provinces are short and pot-bellied.

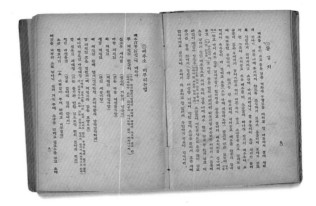

what similar. *Chachae* kimchees are fermented in salt and rice, while *chochae* kimchees are made with fermented fish or shrimp paste, soy sauce, ginger, garlic, and vinegar for a salty, sour and spicy-hot flavor.

All these types of kimchee could be thought of as different kinds of *cho*, but the book sets aside a special *chochae* category for kimchees peculiar to Korea. *Chochae* and *omjangchae* are distinguished by the fact that *chochae* is eaten as is after fermenting while *omjangchae* is reprocessed either by washing it in water first or by adding it to another dish. In *chechae* the vegetables are cut up, while in *chochae* they are generally used whole. *Chochae* kimchees are meant to be kept for a long period of time and are regarded as the mainstream kimchees of Korea.

The book is fairly comprehensive and the recipes are arranged systematically by vegetable and type. Among the many radish kimchees described is *tamjo*, the precursor of today's *tongchimi*, and *hwangajo*, a kimchee made of radish greens. There is also a cabbage kimchee produced by the *tamjopop* or bland method, and a recipe for *muyomji* made without salt. Another useful book was *Tongguk Sesigi*, compiled by Hong Song-Mo in 1849; it describes the preparation of winter kimchi very clearly.

By the early 20th century, many of today's kimchees had come into existence, albeit some with minor alterations. Pang Sin-Yong's 1935 Korean cookbook, *Choson Yori Chepop* (*The Choson Cookery Book*) is the first book that gives detailed explanations, in modern terminology, of how to make kimchee. The types of kimchee identified in *Chungbo Sallim Kyongje* as being common are represented as mainstream varieties in this modern cookbook.

Left: Garlic on sale at a mid-20th-century marketplace.

Above: In about 1934, Pang Shin-Yong, professor of home economics at Ewha Women's College, wrote *Choson Yori Chepop* (*The Choson Cookery Book*), which was revised and reissued in 1952 under the new title *Uri Nara Umsik Mandunun Bop* (*How to Make Korean Food*). The author presents modern methods of reproducing the Korean cuisine she learned from her mother, categorizing the recipes into 'winter kimchees' and 'ordinary kimchees.' This was the first book to cover kimchee-making thoroughly.

Below: An example of a *chabaegi*, a broad, round ceramic bowl used for salting vegetables and mixing spices for seasoning kimchee. This multi-purpose vessel usually had handles and was also used to convey foods from one place to another in the kitchen or for washing dishes.

Above: Kimchee was traditionally stored in different places depending on how long it needed to be fermented and how soon it was to be eaten. A pot of kimchee to be eaten fairly soon would be kept in the shade of the *changtoktae*, an outdoor raised platform. Kimchee to be eaten later in winter was kept inside a specially built storeroom, while crocks of kimchee that were expected to last till spring would be buried in the ground. The storeroom was built of a thick thatch of straw, which allowed proper ventilation while maintaining the temperature and humidity at a fairly constant level. The conical storeroom (known as a *kimcheegwang* or sometimes an *ogari*) in the picture is reminiscent of a yurt.

Above, right: Chilies originally come from central Mexico and were first introduced to Europe by the Portuguese. In kimchee, chili powder helps suppress the propagation of unwanted micro-organisms. Korean chilies are only about one-third as hot as those commonly grown in other countries, but they contain about twice the amount of vitamin C and have 1.2 to 1.5 times as much sweet flavor as they do spicy-hotness.

Cultural Context

As we have seen, the overriding factor in the development of various types of kimchee is this so-called extra taste: pungency. However, it is not only the taste that counts. Koreans were – and still are – very much concerned with the visual and symbolic aspects of food.

In Korean cosmology, the Five Colors of yellow, white, black, red and green are associated with the Five Directions: blues and greens are associated with the east, reds with the south, white with the west, black with the north and yellows and browns with the center. Therefore the Five Colors are associated not only with the directions, but with the four seasons and the change of seasons; in other words, they are symbols of time as well as space. The Five Colors are rooted in the northeast Asian theory of Yin and Yang and the Five Modes of Action (Wood, Fire, Earth, Metal and Water), elements thought to compose all natural and human phenomena.

However, it is not just the sense of color that follows the principles of the Five Modes of Action; the sense of taste does too, with the corresponding flavors being spicy-hot, sweet, sour, salty and bitter. By applying the Five Modes of Action to everyday culinary matters, Koreans created a code of visual and gustatory symbols that mirrored Korean cosmology. Korean food brings together the whole spectrum of colors, shapes and tastes in a balanced harmony or a 'symphony of flavors.'

Of all traditional Korean foods, the one that exhibits this symbolism the most clearly is *ohunch'ae*, a vegetable dish. The *o* part of the name means five, and the *humch'ae* stands for strong herbs such as scallions, garlic and chives, plants that Korean folk tradition regards as possessing cosmic power of harmonizing and blending. At the vernal equinox, the king would grant his retainers gifts of *ohunch'ae*: the herbs would be arranged with the yellow one in the middle and the green, white, red and black ones placed around it in the order corresponding to east, west, south and north. The act of mixing these together and eating them represented the political concept of all the various factions on the outside being

Left: Crocks of a type called *haeju dok*, dating from the latter part of the Choson Dynasty. Though the shapes and other characteristics of kimchee crocks vary from region to region, they are all generally made of earthenware, mostly brown-glazed. The *haeju dok*, however, which come from the Kwanso region (the northwestern part of the peninsula) are unusual in that they are made of porcelain. No one is sure exactly why or when such porcelain crocks were developed, but most extant examples are from late in the Choson Dynasty. In form and decoration, they show the influence of the blue-on-white porcelain tradition; indeed, some examples seem to have been made using identical techniques. A few decades ago it was common to see small white porcelain jars and vases decorated with blue peonies sitting on the rice chest in the wooden floor of a traditional home, adding a touch of elegance to the decor, but in the Kwanso region, better-off families went so far as to have their large crocks made of porcelain. Peonies are the most common motif used on *haeju dok*, but other common motifs include fish and flowers.

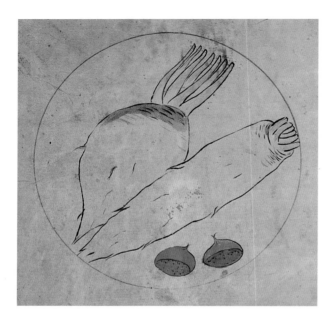

Above: A folk painting by an unknown artist of the Choson Dynasty. The radish was probably introduced to Korea in the 1st century BC.

Above right: The eggplant seems to have originated in southeast Asia or India and probably came to Korea via China some time before the 5th century. It is easily grown; the variety most commonly found in Korea is the long, black-purple type as pictured here.

Far right: A view of a market from more recent times. Cabbage was mentioned in Korean documents as long ago as the Koryo Dynasty, but the cabbage of that period was not popularly eaten because it was small and had a sparse core. Today's cabbage is easy to cultivate, has a pleasant taste, and pickles well, making it the predominant vegetable for use in kimchee. When someone uses the word 'kimchee', cabbage kimchee is generally implied. Cabbages with big, densely packed heads were not grown in Korea until the 1850s.

united under the king (the yellow center). Similarly, in ordinary middle-class households, *ohunch'ae* was eaten during the spring equinox. Here, the Five Colors and Five Flavors had a different significance: green stood for the virtue of benevolence, red for politeness, yellow for fidelity, white for righteousness and black for wisdom (the Five Cardinal Virtues), while green signified the spleen, red the lungs, yellow the heart, white the liver and black the kidneys. Thus, if one ate *ohunch'ae* on the day of the equinox one would acquire all Five Cardinal Virtues and enjoy good health through the balanced and harmonious functioning of all the organs of the body.

There are many such dishes in Korean cookery. For example, *shinsollo* is a stew containing the Five Colors in the form of meat, fish, vegetables, stone mushrooms, walnuts, ginkgo nuts, chestnuts, pine nuts and threads of dried chili. Rainbow rice cakes have multi-colored layers reminiscent of traditional Korean striped garments. Not only are the colors and tastes combined; the sources of the various ingredients also make for a spatial mixture, as they are taken from the fields, the mountains, the sea and even the sky (fowl).

It is not only the dishes themselves that mirror this concept of Korean cosmology. It is also the way that they are eaten. At a Korean meal all the dishes are placed on the table at the same time: the rice, the soup, the vegetables, the meat, the fish and even the rice cakes or *shikhye* which serve as dessert. The meal is distinguished by the number of side dishes – five, seven, or more, and is consumed with a spoon and chopsticks at the same time. The blandness of the rice counteracts the flavors of the meat and fish dishes, and the kimchee clears the palate in order to taste the next dish.

Thus it may be seen that the preparation, the dishes themselves and the consumption of the meal are part and parcel of Korean culture, belief and cosmology. It is believed that the taste of Korean food is the taste of the harmonization of heaven, earth and man. As one eats kimchee, one eats the universe, and in so doing becomes part of the universe and the universe becomes part of man. It is much more than simply sitting down for a meal!

INGREDIENTS: VEGETABLES

Vegetables compose the main 'body' of each individual kimchee. Their freshness and quality are of paramount importance. Make your local Asian grocer the first port of call for kimchee ingredients. Some are a little obscure, in which case substitutions have been suggested.

KOREAN CABBAGE, PAECH'U

Baicai, wong nga bak or ta paak tsai, meaning 'white vegetable,' are all the same. The vegetable has a long shape, like cos lettuce, with closely packed pale green to white leaves. The leaves are very delicate in flavour. There are two types – one with narrower leaves and a longer stem, and the other has broader leaves and is more squat.

GOURD, PAK

Gourds are members of the squash (Cucurbitaceae) family, with a delicately flavoured flesh. Dried gourd strips are also popular in Korea. For gourd kimchee, hollow out the gourd, peel and dice the flesh. Salt, rinse and drain, then season with chili pepper powder and threads of red pepper. Add sliced scallions and pear, and ladle a brine of anchovies over it.

CUCUMBER, OI

A popular vegetable on the Korean table. Cucumber grows well without special fertilization or watering; if you are buying them, choose young, slender varieties, preferably with thin skins. Zucchini is not a substitute.

BELLFLOWER ROOT, TORAJI

Westerners saw a bell in this blue flower and so named it 'bellflower.' Because of their appearance, bellflower and ginseng roots have been symbols of the male. The roots are steeped in brine or rubbed with salt to remove the bitter taste; or tossed in a seasoning of chili pepper powder, leek, and crushed garlic; and fermented. Or they could be processed like kkaktugi, a somewhat dry, diced radish kimchee. Omit if the fresh is not available.

RADISH, MU

Also known by its Japanese name, daikon, Korea is famous for the sheer variety of its radish dishes. Choose firm, unblemished specimens, if possible with some greenery attached, which is edible. Scrub well before grating or slicing for use raw in salads or pickle whole.

EGGPLANT, KAJI,

Eggplant is thought to have originated in Southeast Asia and India, and is also used in Korean recipes. Use slender (Japanese) eggplants, not the bulbous variety – the seeds are too large and they need salting before they can be used.

LEEK, P'A

Traditionally, leek was eaten with raw fish in spring and Indian mustard in winter; today, it is still an indispensible ingredient in fish dishes, as it neutralizes the fishy taste and removes harmful elements. Choose leeks that are firm, and wash them carefully to remove all the grit.

LETTUCE, SANGCH'U

The word sangch'u seems to have originated from saengch'ae, 'raw vegetable,' from the fact that it is usually eaten raw. Any soft-leafed lettuce may be used, for instance butter, mignonette or coral.

DRIED RADISH OR CABBAGE LEAVES, SHIRAEGI

The outer cabbage leaves and radish stalks left over from making kimchee are also dried for use in the colder months for a variety of dishes, including shiraegi-kuk, a soup made with soybean paste and the dried leaves, a staple in ordinary Korean households. May be available in packets from good Asian grocers.

KOREAN WATERCRESS, MINARI

A seasonal garden green highly prized by Korean people for its taste, its crunchy texture, and its fragrance. Unless you know someone who has grown minari from seed, you'll have to use western-style watercress, which is more readily available. Wash and dry well before using.

KOREAN LETTUCE SSUMBAGWI

Korea is perhaps the only country to enjoy kimchee made of bitter ssumbagwi and kodulppaegi (Ixeris sonchifolia, a variety of lettuce). For an inauthentic substitute, try other bitter leaves such as curly endive (frisée) or rocket (arugula).

CHIVES, PUCH'U

Chives are known to have come from the northwestern part of China. Use the flat-leafed Chinese variety as far as possible. The conventional chive is a reasonable substitute, but doesn't hold as well as the flat-leafed variety.

INGREDIENTS: SEASONINGS AND PICKLED FISH

The seasonings and pickled fish and fish pastes are the
ingredients that are used to stuff the vegetables in kimchee.
During the fermentation process, it is these vital
ingredients that produce the variety of flavors
that make kimchee so distinctive.

GINGER, SAENGGANG
*The taste of ginger is harmonious
with most vegetables, and improves
the flavor of food but does not spoil
its original flavor. It is a popular
seasoning of various kimchees. Use
young ginger, and peel before using.*

CHILI, KOCH'U
*A pungent spice that prevents the
acidification of vegetables and the
deterioration of lipids in pickled
fish, it gives most kimchee their
distinctive red color. Koch'ujang
('red pepper paste') – known as
Korean chili bean paste, available
in jars from good Asian grocers –
is made by fermenting soybean paste
and red pepper powder.*

GARLIC, MANUL
*Old Chinese books record that garlic
was first brought to China during
the Han Dynasty. The Korean prize
garlic for its powerful smell and
sharp taste. Choose firm heads
(quorms).*

WILD ROCAMBOLE, TALLAE
*A plant (Allium monanthum)
that used to grow all over China,
which the Chinese called xiaosuan,
'small garlic.' Wild rocambole has
been known to be a therapeutic
plant from the earliest times. People
enjoyed seasoned wild rocambole,
wild rocambole kimchee, and wild
rocambole kkaktugi. Omit if
not available.*

INDIAN MUSTARD, KAT
*In general, kat, or Indian mustard,
is like mustard seed, a variety of
the Brassica juncea family. Use the
brownish or reddish-brown seeds,
available from Indian and Asian
grocers and stores.*

SALT, SOGUM

Most Koreans eat a mainly vegetarian diet and need more sodium than meat eaters. Use coarse sea salt for making kimchee unless otherwise specified. Salt is also an important element in fermentation, and contributes a 'tertiary' taste, a more complex flavour, to dishes.

PICKLED SHRIMP, SAEUJOT

Pickled shrimps are one of the earliest pickled foods in Korea and are much prized. They have a very strong and pungent smell, and are sold in glass jars. Use as a condiment.

SPONGY SEAWEED (GLUE PLANT), CH'ONGGAK

A maritime algae that has a rich fragrance and a pleasant crunchy texture. It grows on rocks to be as thick as wire and as long as seven to ten centimeters. Because it branches like antlers, it is called ch'onggakch'ae or nokkakch'ae, 'green antler seaweed.' It is usually bought dried and then soaked in water for cooking. A dash of vinegar gives it a liveliness. Spongy seaweed is indispensable in juicy kimchees. It completely dispels the fishy smell of pickled fish and neutralizes the smell of garlic and the taste of excessively strong spices. It enriches the spiciness and fragrance of kimchee and takes away the aftertaste.

PICKLED AND SPICED OYSTERS, ORIGULJOT

Oyster dishes in Korea date back to the very earliest times. Today, they are eaten raw or fermented. Since the introduction of chili, Koreans have made origuljot, or salted oysters spiced with red-pepper powder and varied seasonings.

PICKLED SQUID, OJINGOJOT

The ten-tentacled squid is also a popular ingredient in kimchee-making. Choose from dried or fresh varieties.

PICKLED CORBINA, CHOGIJOT

There are about 13,000 kinds of fish in the world, of which about 350 kinds find their way to the dinner table. Koreans eat 150 kinds, and hold the corbina in high regard. Salted corbina has also greatly contributed to the development of the art of fermenting kimchee. While not authentic, other varieties of salted fish will do at a pinch.

PICKLED FISH, CHOTKAL

There are many kinds of pickled fish in East Asia, for instance the nuoc mam of Vietnam, jakt of Borneo, and sossuru of Japan. Korean pickled fish is similarly prized by aficionados. If you can't find the Korean variety, or if you find the taste and smell too strong, try looking for a milder Thai or Vietnamese brand at an Asian grocer.

THE SECRETS OF MAKING KIMCHEE

Hwang Hai-Sung, Korea's master chef of royal court cuisine once said: "The taste of kimchee depends on the hands that made it." This is true of all dishes, but in the case of kimchee the way the hands are used plays a most essential role at every stage of the process.

THE SCIENCE OF MAKING KIMCHEE

The fermentation process that is crucial in the making of kimchee depends on the temperature and air composition of the natural environment, the seasonings used on the ingredients, and the activities of the various micro-organisms that grow in the mixture.

Salt is used in every kind of kimchee. The amount used depends on the region and the season, on individual and family tastes, and eating habits. Salt prevents spoilage, and selectively encourages the growth of beneficial micro-organisms. It also kills the living cells of the vegetables, causing an exchange of materials between the cells, and promotes enzymatic action, which gives the vegetable mix its overall flavor. The magnesium chloride in sea salt causes the pectins in the vegetables to harden, giving the kimchee that crispy chewiness which is one of its special charms. Refined salt, or 'table salt,' will not do for making kimchee and other pickled dishes.

Kimchee has to be weighted down during fermentation. Weighting speeds the effect of salting, draws out the juices of the vegetables more quickly, and prevents contact with the air. This ensures that the vegetables do not wither and lose their crispness.

Kimchee can be largely divided into two categories, according to the method and purpose of production. The 'quick' type depends solely on the physical combination of vegetables and seasonings, and includes kimchee made for immediate consumption and those meant to be kept and eaten over a short period of time. The other group encompasses all the kimchees that are to be stored and eaten over a long period of time and that undergo a fermentation process.

Quick kimchees are essentially 'raw.' They are made by simply adding seasonings and ingredients to the vegetables to kill un-wanted micro-organisms and to create the desired flavor. The first stage of making these 'instant' kimchees is the same as for the fermented: the vegetables are salted to create an osmotic pressure differential that draws the moisture out of the cells and retards their breakdown, preventing mushiness and spoilage. Quick kimchee lacks the special flavors that emerge in the long process of fermentation and does not keep well.

When kimchee pickled in salt is allowed to mature, at first its flavor is merely salty and nothing more, but with the passage of time and ongoing fermentation, sour and slightly sweet tastes are released. This fermented, mature flavor (or, more precisely, pungency) is a result of the beneficial micro-organisms spreading and doing their job; it is the integrated flavourings and seasonings that give kimchee its characteristic taste.

Just because the vegetables that go into the kimchee have been sliced, does not mean that their cells have died. They continue to live for some time afterward, and as long as they are alive, the salinity of the brine they are immersed in cannot penetrate their walls and the seasonings are not absorbed. This gives the resulting dish a mere surface seasoning and an unevenness of flavor that is typical of the dishes called *much'im* in Korean and of certain kimchees made quickly for immediate consumption. After a while, however, the osmotic pressure of the brine draws the water from inside the cells and they die. From this point on, the seasonings penetrate into the vegetable tissues, and in the ensuing exchange of fluids between the interior and exterior cells, the tissues become more tender and the flavor more even. The vegetable cells can also be killed by scalding, or by allowing them to wilt in the shade, but salting is faster. Thus, kimchees made by salting can be eaten right away, before fermentation has taken place.

Although lactic acid is the primary acid produced during kimchee fermentation, other acids are also formed in the process. These include non-volatile succinic acid, manganese butyrate, and propionic acid. The special flavor and smell of fully ripe kimchee is the result of the chemical actions and reactions of these substances. Science has yet to completely understand the chemistry of these reactions and the compounds they produce, so it is not yet possible to artificially recreate their taste. Similarly, there are no chemical substitutes for fermented foods such as vinegar, brewed alcoholic drinks, fermented condiments and sauces, and pickled seafood.

Another contributor to the unique flavors of kimchee comes from the breakdown of the proteins in some of the seasonings used. The pickled fish and shrimp used in some kimchees are made up of protein derivatives, and just a little of such pickled condiments go a long way in affecting the taste of kimchee.

Kimchee tastes best when the yeasts in it have produced esters and blocked the growth of harmful microorganisms. After this point, as the lactic acid bacteria propagate further, the alcohol and carbohydrates are consumed and the kimchee gradually turns sour and spoils. Therefore, it is good to block excessive development of lactic acid bacteria by ventilating the kimchee appropriately during fermentation.

Producing kimchee in large quantities demands careful attention to all the factors that may affect the maturation process. At facilities that mass-produce kimchee, special equipment delivers the right amount of oxygen to the kimchee containers to retard spoilage. However, many manufacturers experience difficulties because of differences between the theory of making kimchee and the actual practice. For these manufacturers, there is still a lot to learn.

PREPARING KIMCHEE

Cultivating

The Korean word for the verb 'to cultivate' was originally used to describe human behavior such as self-grooming. This is symbolic in more ways than one – Koreans take care of their vegetables with as much devotion as they nurture their own children.

It was generally believed that the more care was given, the faster and better the vegetables grew, and the more tasty they would become. This belief has been passed down from one generation to another. For instance, the work of sowing was not delegated to just anyone. According to the kinds of vegetables to be sowed or transplanted, the most prolific woman in the neighborhood or a proud father with many sons was employed, and paid a handsome wage. Farmers sprayed water in dry weather and dug appropriate channels to control the flow of rainwater on wet days. They wrapped certain fields with straw coverings and screens in the cold winter and provided shade for crops in the sunny, hot summer. Hardened soil was crushed, and extra cover was provided when the soil was thin. If the wind blew strong and long branches hung loose, farmers set up supports and tied the vegetables to them. It was – and is – a labour of love.

Initial Preparation

Korean people believe that food begins to acquire its flavor from the moment the cook begins to prepare the ingredients. In the old days, it was said that experienced housewives could distinguish the taste of a vegetable trimmed by hand from one trimmed in other ways. In the process of preparing such vegetables as spinach,

Indian mustard leaves, and Korean watercress, as well as bean sprouts, it is necessary to remove rotten leaves, roots, and foreign matter one by one, by hand. Treating even the smallest ingredients with care is thought to make the dish taste that much better. It was an unconscious Korean assumption that living vegetable crops should not be harmed in any way. Not only did people avoid the use of a knife, they were also careful not to let their fingernails dig into any part of the plant. If the leaves of a vegetable were too big to eat, they were torn by hand rather than cut with a knife, lest the taste be altered. Koreans of old thought that a vegetable cut by a knife bled, just like a human body does, and therefore lost its taste.

Washing

Korean women, in times past, would begin their day by drawing water from the well. First they would clean themselves, then set about cleaning their house, children and the food that they were to prepare that day. It was, and still is, very important to clean the raw ingredients of Korean food because many of them, especially the vegetables, are eaten raw or just scalded briefly. Therefore, all vegetables are washed at least three times and rinsed repeatedly in fresh water. There was a saying that the housewife that didn't wash her vegetables three times would not be able to bear a son. Thus, the cleansing was a ritual process, as much as it was a practical one.

Slicing

In the past, Koreans avoided slicing vegetables with a metal knife whenever possible. The custom of avoiding slicing was perhaps derived from the philosophy of not destroying the original form of food ingredients. They also believed that vegetables would not taste so good if sliced using a metal knife. In the kitchens of the royal household, knives of bamboo rather than metal were used to slice and pare Korean radishes. Garlic and ginger were never sliced with a knife, but were pressed or crushed. Chilies were ground in a stone mortar. It was a principle that in every kind of kimchee the vegetables should be pickled whole. According to Korean folklore, fermentation was a process controlled by God. If any of the ingredients were touched by things made of metal, God would be angry or displeased and would spoil the process.

Even when the time came to eat the pickled kimchee, Koreans avoided slicing it with a knife, thinking it might spoil the taste. Instead, they tore or pulled the kimchee apart by hand. Korean radish and cucumber kimchees were sliced lengthwise, and cabbage kimchee torn off leaf by leaf.

Grinding

Just as Korean people could tell the difference in taste between foods sliced with a knife and those torn by hand, they could also tell the difference between the taste of chilies ground by hand and those ground with a mortar or other grinding implement. They used one or the other method depending on the type of food being prepared. Big mortars were used for pounding barley and other grains, but the smaller ones served to grind up such seasonings as garlic, sesame seeds, and ginger. Sometimes large, natural rocks were placed in the courtyard near the well and hollowed out to be used as mortars for crushing or grinding chilies. When the hollow became worn very deep after long use, it was put to use as the mortar for a much larger pestle attached to a treadle. Even when chilies were ground in a stone mortar, Koreans divided them

into various categories, some to be ground a number of times with the stone turned clockwise, some with the stone counter-clockwise, some with pressure from the elbows, the shoulders or from the waist depending on the level of grinding; sometimes a combination of some or all of the above were employed.

To pickle the young leafy summer radish kimchee, chilies were ground. If sliced or crushed chilies were used, the kimchee sours too soon. The manner in which the rice is prepared is also said to affect the acidification.

Salting

When making kimchee, salting is not a simple matter of merely placing the cabbages, radishes or other vegetables in salted water – in olden times women carefully selected a day free of inauspicious influences to salt the vegetables to be pickled for winter. They would prepare themselves for seven days in advance; this preparation (or purification) rite differed from region to region.

Salting is a process that allows the seasoning to penetrate the food gradually. Today, salting is done in one day; in the past, it took place over a period of three, five, seven, or even nine days. The vegetables were moved from container to container of salted water, each with a brine solution of a different strength. It was considered that the longer the process took and the slower the salt was absorbed, the deeper the taste of the kimchee. Cabbages were not salted in volume, nor were they salted one at a time. The quantity of salt and the way of salting varied according to which part of the cabbage was being seasoned. More and a richer brine was used on the thick parts near the root, and salt inserted between each layer of leaves.

Seasoning

The secret of the taste of kimchee is the various combinations of seasonings used during fermentation. Seasoning is the process of stuffing the main ingredients with various seasonings, which, as the pickle ferments, will perform their magic on the salted vegetables. In the case of cabbage kimchee, the most used sea-sonings, in order of popularity, are: chili, salt, garlic, scallions and ginger, fermented baby shrimp paste and fresh oysters, Indian mustard leaf and carrots, sugar and fermented yellow corbina paste, fermented anchovy paste, sponge seaweed, shrimp, and sesame, pollack, and octopus. Their use differs according to time, region and family.

Different combinations of seasonings, quantity and quality, create the various tastes and individual characteristics of kimchee. The taste is also affected by the temperature at which the kimchee is fermented, and the ratio of salt and water used in the salting. Garlic, anchovies, and especially chili quicken fermentation, while scallions, ginger, and the like do not affect it much.

Fermenting

The unique fermented taste of Korean food results from a kind of 'controlled spoilage.' Before the introduction of chilies, vegetables were fermented in brine flavoured with Japanese pepper and fennel. With the advent of chilies, Korean cooks found that the active compound that gives the chili its characteristic hotness – capsaicin – delays the acidification process in kimchee production. This unique fermented taste is produced just before acidification. The chilies therefore produce this taste and also preserve the delicious taste of kimchee.

Storing

Kimchee's fermenting phase, which goes on for some time, is followed by a phase of turning sour. This acidification is slowed down or delayed for a comparably long time by storing the kimchee in large earthenware jars. Korean earthenware is made of clay, which is very low in heat conductivity, and does not heat up or cool off easily. It is not very thick and heavy, but it preserves heat with great efficiency. It effectively insulates the kimchee against the outside temperatures, cold or hot, and maintains a steady temperature inside. Ideally, kimchee should be stored at temperatures below zero Celsius, but if the temperature can be held at four degrees continuously, the acidification of the kimchee can be delayed for as long as three months. In traditional Korean homes, a large earthenware jar placed in the shade keeps the kimchee at an optimum temperature.

The acidification of kimchee is caused by the action of microbes. One method of artificially preventing the action of microbes in kimchee is to boil it, as microbes are killed by heat. But it is vital that kimchees have the texture of a fresh vegetable when chewed, and boiling alters the texture of the food. Another method of preventing souring is to use chemicals that prevent the growth of microbes. But a lot of 'antibiotics' would be necessary since there are many kinds of microbes in kimchee. The third method is to store kimchee in a refrigerator, a method used by big kimchee manufacturers. For the kimchees in this book, it is recommended that you place the kimchee in an earthenware crock (never ever use metal), cover it with a tight-fitting lid or plastic wrap, and refrigerate it in the crisper section of the refrigerator or in the coolest part of your kitchen.

Burying

The climate of the Korean peninsula is affected by masses of hot air from the South Pacific during summer and by masses of cold air from Siberia during winter. Changes in temperature are the main cause of deterioration of food. Burying takes advantage of the earth's insulating effect, and maximizes the length of time kimchee can be kept without losing its flavor. In the past, perishables and grain were stored in a warehouse built in the ground. Since its earthen floor, walls, and ceiling shut off the temperature changes of the outside air, one feels a coolness and freshness upon entering a traditional warehouse. In the past, Koreans stored their kimchee, in different places depending on when it was to be eaten. They placed the jars of kimchee on the terrace in the shade if it was to be eaten quickly; in the earthen warehouse if it was to be eaten later in the winter; and buried the jars in the earth if the kimchee was to be dug out in the winter and eaten in the spring.

Covering

Straw is a highly suitable traditional material for storing vegetables thanks to its excellent ability to keep temperature and humidity constant while providing adequate ventilation. In Korea, several straw coverings were scattered over the backyard during winter. They were also used to cover the buried jars of kimchee and vegetables. Rich families built straw cabins to store their kimchees in the proper temperature. Koreans lived out their lives under the protection of straw, surrounded by it, enjoying the food it covered, and when they died, their bodies were buried in the earth, tied up with straw ropes, and laid on a straw mat in the coffin. In the modern world, and with the advent of appliances, the straw is optional!

MAKING KIMCHEE AT HOME

The recipes in this book are divided into Winter, Spring, Summer, Autumn and Year-Round Kimchees, because traditionally the dishes were prepared at particular times of the year. Today, however, with increased availability of products, most of these dishes may be made year round. Nonetheless, whenever the dishes are prepared, there are certain ground rules that must be followed:

1. Never use a reactive metal container to store the kimchee; stainless steel will suffice, but porcelain is best.

2. If using plastic containers for storage, the chilli redness will stain permanently.

3. Store kimchee in a cool dark spot (the back of a cool kitchen cupboard is a good place). Better still, keep it in the fridge.

4. Always cover the container and seal well before allowing the fermentation processes to begin.

5. The recipes are offered in as traditional a manner as is possible, so beware of the variants in temperature. If making kimchee in the tropics or in a mediterranean climate, you will need to adjust temperature controls!

6. The specified amounts of chili and chili powders err on the side of generous in this book; adjust according to personal taste.

7. Many of the recipes use rice porridge; when making rice porridge, use this recipe for 1 quantity ($1/2$ cup or 125 ml): dissolve 1 tablespoon rice flour in $3/4$ cup water; bring to the boil, and cool.

WINTER KIMCHEE RECIPES

Recipes for the more robust and pungent kimchees can be found here. These flavours help to cut across the richness and heartiness of heavy winter fare such as slow-cooked casseroles and hotpots, noodle soups and grilled meats. These kimchees also make use of fresh, salted or preserved seafood – a virtue born of necessity due to the harsh Korean winters.

STUFFED AND WRAPPED VEGETABLE KIMCHEE
POSSAM KIMCHI
(From previous page)

This is a kimchee that does not keep for a long time, because the fermentation process is light and short. The kimchee is prepared in wrapped bundles, and is stuffed with an unconventional collection of ingredients.

1 small fresh octopus, cut into
    1 in (2.5 cm) pieces
12 fresh oysters or small shrimp, peeled
1/4 cup dried cloud's ear mushrooms
2 large Napa cabbages, about 5 lb (2.5 kg)
1 radish, 1 lb (500 g), finely diced
7 oz (200 g) coarse sea salt
1 gallon (5 liters) water
2 cups scallions, cut into 1 1/2 in (4 cm) lengths
1 cup Korean watercress (minari), cut into
    1 1/4 in (4 cm) lengths
1/2 cup Indian mustard leaves (green),
    cut into 1 1/2 in (4 cm) lengths
1/3 cup julienned garlic
1/4 cup julienned ginger
1/4 cup red hot chili flakes
1/2 cup fish sauce
1 Korean pear (nashi), peeled and finely diced
1 oz (30 g) pine nuts
1/3 cup chestnuts, boiled, peeled and
    julienned
5 Korean or Chinese red dates, seeded and
    julienned
1/4 cup chili threads
1 medium-sized carrot, finely diced

1. Sprinkle the octopus and oysters with salt, and stand for 30 minutes. Drain.
2. Soak the dried mushrooms in hot water for 1 hour until soft. Drain, trim off the hard stalks, and slice into thin juliennes.
3. Trim and discard the discolored outer leaves of the cabbage. Cut it in half lengthwise from the top down 1/3 of the length toward the root end. Hold both parts of the cabbage firmly and pull it in half. Repeat the process with the remaining cabbage. Remove 1/2 of the outer cabbage leaves and set aside. Cut the inner leaves and core into 1 in (2.5 cm) lengths.
4. To make the brine, dissolve 5 oz (140 g) salt in the water. Soak the whole and cut cabbage leaves in the brine overnight or for 14–16 hours. Cover the container with a saucer to completely immerse the vegetables. Drain and rinse under cold water. Drain again.
5. To make the stuffing, gently toss together the scallions, minari, mustard leaves, garlic, ginger and chili. Mix the fish sauce, octopus, oysters or shrimp, together and add to the scallion mixture.
6. To make the garnish, combine the pear, pine nuts, mushroom, chestnuts, dates, chili threads, and carrot. Set aside.
7. Mix the cut cabbage and radish slices with the stuffing and toss gently.
8. Take 4 wilted cabbage leaves and place them crossways on a bowl with the leaf tips pointed outward. Take 1 cup of the stuffing and place in the center of the leaves. Scatter 1 tablespoon of the garnish over the mixture. Then fold over the leaves firmly toward the center into a rounded bundle. Place it neatly into the container to prevent the bundle from falling apart. Cover the bundles with the rest of the cabbage leaves. Prepare a simple brine with the remaining 1 oz (30 g) salt and 1 cup water. Pour it over the bundles. Weight down the kimchee with a small saucer. Cover the lid tightly, then place the container in a cool spot or refrigerator. Ferment the kimchee for 2–3 days, before serving.

TRADITIONAL WHOLE CABBAGE KIMCHEE
T'ONG PAECH'U KIMCHI

This is the most popular type of kimchee throughout the Korean peninsula and has been for many generations. This kimchee is prepared with a combination of herbs, spices, aromatic vegetables, fermented fish or shell-fish sauce, and fresh oysters. The kimchee is assembled and allowed to ferment, which preserves it during the winter months when few fresh vegetables are available.

2–3 fresh and firm-headed whole cabbages,
    about 6 lb (3 kg)
3/4 cup coarse sea salt or kosher salt (granules)
1 gallon (5 liters) water
1 radish, about 1 lb (500 g), julienned
1 cup julienned carrot (optional)
1 quantity rice porridge (page 41)
1/2 cup clear fish sauce or 1/3 cup fermented
    shrimp paste
1 tsp finely ground red pepper powder
1/4 tsp red hot dry chili flakes
1 tsp crushed fresh garlic
1/4 cup fresh ginger, peeled and crushed
10 scallions, cut into 2 in (5 cm) pieces
1 cup Indian mustard leaves, cut into
    2 in (5 cm) pieces (optional)
1 cup Korean watercress (minari), cut into
    2 in (5 cm) lengths (optional)
1/3 cup sponge seaweed, cut into
    2 in (5 cm) lengths (optional)
1/4 cup red dry chili threads

1. Trim and discard the discolored outer leaves of the cabbage. Cut it in half lengthwise from the top down 1/3 of the length toward the root end. Hold both parts of the cabbage firmly and pull it in half. (Do not cut the cabbage all the way through since this will damage the tender, inner leaves, which are the tastiest part. The inner leaves will still be attached to the cabbage core when the cabbage is torn in half.) Repeat

the process with the remaining cabbage.

2. To make the brine, mix the salt with the water in a glass, stone or plastic container. Put the cabbage upright into the container and soak for 16–18 hours or overnight. Rinse the cabbage thoroughly in cold water and drain well.

3. Mix the radish with 1 tablespoon salt to wilt it. Do not rinse.

4. To make the red paste, in a large mixing bowl, put the rice porridge, fish sauce, red pepper powder, red chili flakes, garlic, and ginger paste. Mix with the wilted radish and carrots. Add the scallions, mustard leaves,

watercress, red chili threads, and oysters. Stir gently to mix.

5. Lift up the leaves of the cabbage which are still attached to the core and push a little stuffing between the leaves in a layering process. Do this, using all the stuffing, with all the cabbage. Take two of the flexible outer leaves and fold them around the cabbage halves to wrap the stuffing inside. The leaves on the tip of the cabbage are folded over and tucked into the outer folded-over leaves.

6. Place the stuffed cabbage halves flat in the storage container of your choice with the inner leaves facing up. Keep in a cool, clean, shaded

place or refrigerator to ferment.

7. If the container is not tightly packed, fill the empty space with a light brine made from 1 tablespoon salt dissolved in 1 cup of water. The brine should completely cover the cabbage (do not expose the cabbage to air). Cover, and ferment for 3–4 weeks in a cool place. Sample after 2 weeks to test its strength.

Note: Several ingredients are optional since they are not indispensable to the fermentation of the kimchee, but add an authentic flavour. MSG is popular in Korea and Japan, but its use is controversial elsewhere.

ASSORTED WATERY KIMCHEE
SOKPAK TONGCH'IMI

Cabbage and radish combine here. The technique of assembling this double kimchee is the same as for other watery kimchees.

1 large cabbage, about 2 lb (1 kg)
1–2 radishes, about 2 lb (1 kg), well scrubbed
8 oz (230 g) coarse sea salt
1 gallon (5 liters) water, plus 1 ¹/₂ quarts
    (1.5 liters) for kimchee juice
¹/₃ cup julienned garlic
¹/₄ cup julienned fresh ginger
5 oz (140 g) scallions, well-rinsed and trimmed
3–4 red whole fresh chili
¹/₂ cup spongy seaweed, in 2 in (5 cm) lengths

1. Trim and discard the discolored outer leaves of the cabbage. Cut it in half lengthwise from the top down ¹/₃ of the length toward the root end. Hold both parts of the cabbage firmly and pull it in half. Cut the radish in half from the tip to the root end. Set aside.
2. To make the brine, dissolve 5 oz (140 g) salt in the water. Soak the cabbage and radish halves in the brine for 14–16 hours. Cover the container to immerse the vegetables. Drain and rinse under cold water. Drain again.
3. To make the stuffing, wrap the garlic and ginger in cheesecloth and put into the brine mixture. Divide the scallions, chili and seaweed into two equal parts. Put one part of each scallion mixture on each wilted cabbage half.
4. Place the cut side of each radish half on the cabbage, and wrap two outer leaves of the cabbage around the radish to hold it all together. Place the bundle neatly in the container. Do the same for the other halves and stuffing.
5. Prepare a brine of 1 ¹/₂ quarts (1.5 liters) water and the remaining 3 oz (85 g) salt and pour this into the container. Cover the liquid with a saucer to hold down the bundles. Cover, and ferment for 4–5 weeks in a cool place.

WHOLE CABBAGE WATERY KIMCHEE

T'ONG PAECH'U TONGCH'IMI

Tongch'imi is a traditional midwinter night snack eaten after dinner with noodles.The soaking liquid is often used as a base for cold noodle soup.

1–2 large Napa cabbages, about 4 lb (2 kg)
8 oz (230 g) coarse sea salt
1 gallon (5 liters) water
5 oz (140 g) green chilies, salt-cured
4 oz (115 g) scallions, including roots
2 oz (60 g) spongy seaweed (optional)
2 oz (60 g) julienned garlic
1 oz (30 g) julienned fresh ginger
1 ½ quarts (1.5 liters) water

1. Trim and discard the discolored outer leaves of the cabbage. Cut it in half lengthwise from the top down ⅓ of the length toward the root end. Hold both parts of the cabbage and pull it in half. Repeat with the remaining cabbage.
2. To make the brine, do the same process as on left, but with the cabbage, not the radish.
3. Put 1–2 green chilies on top of the inner small wilted leaves. Fold over the tip of the cabbage to cover the chilies. Take 2 outer leaves and wrap around the cabbage. Tie up the bundle with 2 scallions.
4. Put the spongy seaweed, if used, on the bottom of a container. Neatly arrange the cabbage halves on top.
5. Wrap the garlic and ginger loosely in cheesecloth and place on the cabbage halves. Cover, and allow to stand overnight in a cool spot.
6. Mix the remaining 3 oz (85 g) salt with the water and gently pour it over the radish. Pour over the cabbage (the liquid should fill the container). Cover, and ferment for 2–4 weeks in a cool place.
7. Serve the leaves whole or cut the bundle into bite-sized pieces. Traditionally this kimchee was served with the brine as a cold soup.

WHOLE RADISH WATERY KIMCHEE

T'ONG MU TONGCH'IMI

A kimchee assembled in the same manner as the Whole Cabbage Watery Kimchee (on right). Both vegetables lend themselves admirably to this sort of fermentation.

4 lb (2 kg) radish, well cleaned
8 oz (230 g) coarse sea salt
1 gallon (5 liters) water
4–5 green chilies, salt-cured or fermented
4 oz (115 g) scallions, including roots
2 oz (60 g) spongy seaweed (optional)
⅓ cup julienned garlic
¼ cup julienned fresh ginger
1 ½ quarts (1.5 liters) water

1. Do not peel the radish, but, if possible, retain the green stems and leaves.
2. To make the brine, dissolve 5 oz (140 g) of the salt in the water in a large container. Add the radish to the brine and cover with a plate to make sure they are well immersed. Soak for 16–18 hrs. Drain, rinse with cold water, and drain again.
3. Place 1–2 chilies lengthwise on top of the radish. Fold the radish leaves over the chilies to hold them in place and tie up the bundle with 2 scallions. Repeat with the rest of the radish.
4. Put the spongy seaweed, if used, on the bottom of the container. Neatly arrange the radish bundles on top.
5. Wrap the garlic and ginger loosely in cheesecloth and place in-between the radishes. Cover, and allow to stand overnight in a cool spot.
6. Mix the remaining 3 oz (85 g) salt with the water and gently pour it over the radish. Cover, and let it ferment for 4–5 weeks in a cool, dark place.
7. To serve, cut the radish in half lengthwise and slice thinly. This kimchee is traditionally served cold with the soaking liquid, which is drunk, and sometimes served with noodles.

MIXED WHOLE CABBAGE AND RADISH KIMCHEE
SOKPAK T'ONG KIMCHI

In upper-class homes in times past and sometimes even today, the male members of the family were served their meals first on low individual tables. They were served the first-cut kimchee, neatly arranged as it came from the cutting board. The female members and children were served the second serving or leftover kimchee after the family head had dined – it was unthinkable for women and children to be served first-cut kimchee.

1 large Napa cabbage, about 3 lb (1.5 kg)
3 radishes, about 3 lb (1.5 kg), well scrubbed
8 oz (230 g) coarse sea salt
1 gallon (5 liters) water
1 1/2 quantities rice porridge (page 41)
2/3 cup fish sauce
1/3 cup red hot dry chili flakes
1/4 cup red chili powder
2/3 cup fermented (cured) corvina or squid, chopped
1/3 cup finely chopped garlic
1/4 cup finely chopped fresh ginger
1/3 cup sponge seaweed, cut into
    1 1/2 in (4 cm) pieces (optional)
1/2 cup Indian mustard leaves, cut into
    1 1/2 in (4 cm) lengths
3 scallions, cut into 1 1/2 in (4 cm) lengths
1/2 cup Korean watercress (minari), cut into
    1 1/2 in (4 cm) lengths
1/4 cup dry chili threads

1. Trim and discard the discolored outer leaves of the cabbage. Cut it in half lengthwise from the top down 1/3 of the length toward the root end. Hold both parts of the cabbage firmly and pull it in half. Tear off and reserve several of the outer leaves. Cut the radishes in half lengthwise all the way through.
2. To make the brine, dissolve 6 oz (170 g) salt in the water. Soak the cabbage, radish halves, and the reserved outer leaves in the brine for 14–16 hours or overnight. Cover the container with a saucer to completely immerse the vegetables. Drain and rinse under cold water. Drain again.
3. To make the red paste seasoning, combine the rice porridge, fish sauce, chili flakes and powder, corvina, ginger, and garlic into a mixing bowl. Toss and mix well. Add the seaweed, mustard leaves, scallions, minari, and chili threads. Toss all the ingredients together gently and thoroughly.
4. Take the wilted cabbage halves and cut them in half lengthwise. Place the seasoning between the leaves. Take 2 outer leaves that are still attached to the core and wrap them around the cabbage to hold it all together. Place in the container with one half of a radish facing the cut side of the cabbage. Place the extra radish pieces on top of the cabbage and place the reserved outer leaves over the vegetables as a protective cover.
5. Sprinkle the remaining 2 oz (60 g) salt over the vegetables. Cover tightly and ferment in the crisper section of your refrigerator for 3–4 weeks.
6. To serve, place the cabbage and radish on a cutting board. Cut the cabbage into 1 1/2 in (4 cm) wide pieces and place neatly in a serving dish. Cut the radish into 1/4 in (0.5 cm) slices. The cabbage and radish should not look jumbled: this is considered rude.

FROZEN POLLACK PICKLE
TONGT'AE SHIKHAE

Pollack is a lean fish with very little fat. Since it is caught in deep waters away from port, the fish is cleaned and frozen on board the ship. This pickle can therefore be prepared throughout the year. It was, however, a winter specialty for many generations. You can use orange roughy in place of the pollack.

7 oz (200 g) sea salt
3 lb (1.5 kg) pollack fillets
3 oz (85 g) red chili powder
3 lb (1.5 kg) radish, cut into 3 in (7.5 cm) pieces
1 lb (500 g) cooked millet
3 oz (85 g) chopped garlic
2 oz (60 g) chopped ginger
4 oz (115 g) fish sauce
1 quantity rice porridge (page 41)
1 oz (30 g) red hot chili flakes
8 oz (230 g) scallions, halved lengthwise,
    cut into 3 in (7.5 cm) lengths

1. Rub 4 oz (115 g) salt into the fillets. Cover tightly with plastic wrap and weight down with a plate. Leave to stand for 2 days in the refrigerator. Cut the fish into bite-sized (1 1/2 in/4 cm) pieces. Rub with the chili powder. Set aside in a cool place.
2. Toss the radish with 1 oz (30 g) salt. Allow to stand in a cool place.
3. To make the seasoning, combine the millet, garlic, ginger, fish sauce, rice porridge, chili flakes, and remaining 2 oz (60 g) salt. Mix with the fish, radish, and scallions. Put into a sealable container and allow to mature for 2–3 weeks. This kimchee is usually served as a side dish at a traditional Korean meal.

DRIED POLLACK KIMCHEE
TONGT'AE SOKPAKCHI

This is a short-term specialty kimchee for all seasons. If pollack is unavailable, choose a fish with very little fat, for an inauthentic substitute.

4 lb (2 kg) dried pollack
3 lb (1.5 kg) radish, cut into 1 in (2.5 cm) cubes
3 oz (85 g) salt
3 oz (85 g) chopped garlic
2 oz (60 g) chopped ginger
4 fl oz (115 ml) fish sauce
1/2 quantity rice porridge (page 41)
1 oz (30 g) red hot chili flakes
3 oz (85 g) red chili powder
1 oz (30 g) castor sugar
8 oz (230 g) Korean watercress (minari), cut into 1 1/2 in (4 cm) strips
4 oz (115 g) scallions, cut into 1 1/2 in (4 cm) strips
2 oz (60 g) chestnuts, boiled, peeled and sliced, or 2 oz (60 g) pine nuts
1 oz (30 g) red chili threads

1. Soak the whole pollack in cold water for 30 minutes. Lightly squeeze out the liquid. Set aside. Cut into 1 in (2.5 cm) cubes.
2. Toss the radish with 1 oz (30 g) salt, and stand for 30 minutes. Drain and squeeze lightly.
3. To make the seasoning, combine the garlic, ginger, fish sauce, rice porridge, chili flakes and powder, sugar, and the remaining salt.
4. Gently toss together the pollack, radish, minari, scallions, chestnuts and chili threads. Toss with the seasoning thoroughly, then place in a container. Cover and store in a cool place as a short-term kimchee or serve immediately with a dash of white vinegar.

OCTOPUS KIMCHEE
NAKCHI SOKPAKCHI

This kimchee is both an autumn and winter specialty.

3 lb (1.5 kg) fresh octopus, tentacles only, cut into 1 in (2.5 cm) pieces
6 oz (170 g) salt
4 lb (2 kg) radish, cut into 1 in (2.5 cm) cubes
15 radish leaves and stems
3 oz (85 g) chopped garlic
2 oz (60 g) chopped ginger
4 fl oz (115 ml) fish sauce
1 quantity rice porridge (page 41)
1 oz (30 g) red hot chili flakes
3 oz (85 g) red chili powder
4 oz (115 g) scallions, cut into 2 in (5 cm) lengths
2 oz (60 g) chestnuts, boiled, peeled and sliced
1 oz (30 g) red chili threads

1. Toss the cut octopus with 2 oz (60 g) salt in a container. Cover with plastic wrap and weight down with a plate. Allow it to stand in a cool place for 2–3 hours. (Salting gives the octopus a chewier texture. Or you can blanch the octopus in rapidly boiling water, then rinse in cold water and drain.)
2. Toss the radish, and the leaves and stems with 2 oz (60 g) salt and stand for 30 minutes.
3. To make the seasoning, combine the garlic, ginger, fish sauce, rice porridge, chili flakes and powder, and the remaining 2 oz (60 g) salt. Lightly squeeze out and drain the liquid from the octopus and radish, and mix them with the seasoning. Add the scallions, chestnuts and chili threads. Mix together gently, and transfer the mixture to a sealed container.
4. Allow the mixture to mature for 2–3 days in a cool place before serving.

SQUID AND RADISH KIMCHEE
OJINGO SOKPAKCHI

Semi-dried squid is readily available in Korea and has a firm, chewy texture. Semi-dried radish strips, whether prepared in the home or bought, are the size of the little finger. The unusual dried leaves from the hot chili plant are spinach-like and not pungent like the chili itself.

3 lb (1.5 kg) small semi-dried squid, about 5 in (12.5 cm) long
3 lb (1.5 kg) semi-dried radish
1 lb (500 g) dried hot chili leaves
3 oz (85 g) chopped garlic
2 oz (60 g) chopped ginger
4 fl oz (115 ml) fish sauce
2 oz (60 g) red chili powder
1 oz (30 g) castor sugar
1 oz (30 g) red chili threads
4 oz (115 g) scallions, cut into 2 in (5 cm) pieces

1. Cut the squid with a pair of scissors into 2 in (5 cm) long pieces as thick as your little finger.
2. Soak the squid, radish, and chili leaves in cold water for 30 minutes. Lightly squeeze out the liquid and drain.
3. To make the seasoning, combine the garlic, ginger, fish sauce, chili flakes and powder, and sugar. Toss this with the squid, radish, chili leaves, chili threads, and scallions.
4. Put the kimchee into a container, cover and store in a cool place. Serve immediately with a dash of vinegar and toasted sesame seeds.

STUFFED WHOLE COD KIMCHEE
T'ONG TAEGU KIMCHI

This is a specialty kimchee that emphasizes the preservation of the whole stuffed fish. Usually 10 to 20 whole cod are preserved to be eaten during the 3– to 4–month cold season. Here, the whole cod is stuffed and cut into 4 parts.

5 lb (2.5 kg) fresh cod, left whole
8 oz (230 g) coarse sea salt
1/3 cup crushed garlic
1/4 cup crushed fresh ginger
1/2 cup red hot chili powder or to taste
1/4 cup red hot chili flakes or to taste
3/4 cup fish sauce
2 radishes, about 2 lb (1 kg), julienned
4 scallions, cut into 2 in (5 cm) lengths
1/2 cup *minari*, cut into 2 in (5 cm) lengths

1. Scale and rinse the cod. Make an incision from the head to the tail to open the fish from the back rather than the belly. The opening should reach the belly so that the fish can be spread open to remove the innards. Sprinkle the cod inside and out with 4 oz (115 g) salt.
2. To make the stuffing, combine the garlic, ginger, chili powder and flakes, fish sauce, and 2 oz (60 g) salt. Mix the radish, scallions, *minari* and toss with the seasonings. Stuff the fish full. Cut the fish into 4 equal parts, and place it in a container and cover. Keep covered and ferment for a minimum of 4 weeks in a cool spot.
3. If you like, rinse the fish intestines, liver and roe (if any) with cold water. Remove and discard the bitter green sac. Mix the intestines with the last 2 oz (60 g) salt and place in the container.
4. To serve, remove the cod as needed. Keep the remaining pieces of fish covered with the preserved innards. When the fish is finished, cut the preserved intestines into 1/2 in (1 cm) bits and mix with the soaking liquid. It may be served as a side dish with seasonings such as scallions, sesame seeds and oil.

CURED COD WITH CABBAGE AND RADISH KIMCHEE
TAEGU SOKPAKCHI

Cod is expensive in Korea, so this kimchee has considerable prestige. The cod is pre-salted, so the fermentation process takes less time. It is served like a large, jumbled salad.

1 Napa cabbage, about 3 lb (1.5 kg)
1 radish, about 1 lb (500 g)
8 oz (230 g) coarse sea salt
1 gallon (5 liters) water
1 1/2 quantities rice porridge (page 41)
1/3 cup fish sauce
1/4 cup red hot chili flakes
2/3 cup red chili powder
3 lb (1.5 kg) cured cod, cut in 1 1/2 in (4 cm) cubes
1/3 cup finely chopped garlic
1/4 cup finely chopped ginger
2 cups scallions, cut into 1 1/2 in (4 cm) lengths

Note: To cure or pre-salt the cod, sprinkle the fillet with 1 1/2 oz (45 g) coarse sea salt. Cover and allow to stand, refrigerated, for 2 days.

1. Trim and discard the discolored outer leaves of the cabbage. Remove 3–4 outer leaves from the cabbage and set aside. Cut it in half lengthwise from the top down 1/3 of the length toward the root end. Hold both parts of the cabbage and pull it in half. Cut the cabbage into 3–4 in (7.5–10 cm) lengths. Cut the radish in half and into 3–4 in (7.5–10 cm) lengths.
2. To make the brine, dissolve 5 oz (140 g) salt in the water. Soak the cabbage, radish and outer leaves in the brine for 16–18 hours. Cover the container to completely immerse the vegetables. Drain and rinse under cold water. Drain again.
3. To make the seasoning, mix the porridge, fish sauce, chili flakes and powder in a mixing bowl. Add the cod and mix. Add the garlic, ginger, scallions, cabbage, and radish. Toss the mixture thoroughly. Put it all into a container, cover with the reserved cabbage leaves and sprinkle with the remaining salt. Cover, and ferment for 3 weeks in a cool spot. As the kimchee matures, liquid will accumulate, filling the container. Drain off if necessary.
4. To serve, pile the vegetables and cod into a serving bowl.

WILD LETTUCE KIMCHEE
KODULPPAEGI KIMCHI

The *kodulppaegi* is a dark-green, tough-textured, wild leafy vegetable that looks like spinach, and grows in the southern part of Korea and on Cheju Island. It has a bitter taste and is reputed to assist digestion. This kimchee is usually prepared in the fall for serving in the winter.

4 lb (2 kg) *kodulppaegi* , whole, or spinach
9 oz (255 g) salt
1 gallon (5 liters) water
2 lb (1 kg) radish
6 oz (170 g) scallions, cut into half lengthwise
6 oz (170 g) fermented anchovy paste
1 quantity rice porridge (page 41)
3 oz (85 g) chopped garlic
2 oz (60 g) chopped ginger
3 oz (85 g) red hot chili flakes
2 oz (60 g) red chili powder
4 oz (115 g) chopped fermented squid or
    baby corvina (optional)

1. Rinse, clean and trim the whole *kodulppaegi*. If using spinach, clean well.
2. Prepare a brine with 6 oz (170 g) salt and the water. Submerge the *kodulppaegi* in the brine for 2 days, keeping it well covered, to reduce the bitterness. Rinse, drain and discard the brine.
3. Cut the radish into batons about 1 ½ in (4 cm) long and ¼ in (6 mm) thick. Toss with 1 oz (30 g) salt. Wipe off the salt and moisture, and dry the slices in a basket in a ventilated area but not in direct sunlight. The radish is to remain white.
4. To make the seasoning, combine the anchovy paste, rice porridge, garlic, ginger, chili flakes and powder, the remaining salt, and fermented squid, if using. Mix well and gently toss through the *kodulppaegi*, radish, and scallions. Place in a container, seal and ferment in a cool, dark place for 4–5 weeks.

STUFFED WHOLE RADISH KIMCHEE
T'ONG MU SOBAEGI

A solid-fleshed radish does not lend itself to stuffing as would individual cabbage leaves. Yet the Koreans, in this extremely artful kimchee, have devised a method of stuffing one half of a radish with unique flavors.

4 radishes, about 7 lb (3.5 kg), well scrubbed
8 oz (230 g) coarse sea salt
1 gallon (5 liters) water
2 quantities rice porridge (page 41)
$^2/_3$ cup fish sauce
$^1/_3$ cup red hot chili powder
$^1/_3$ cup red hot chili flakes
$^1/_4$ cup red chili threads
$^2/_3$ cup julienned garlic
$^1/_3$ cup julienned ginger
4 scallions, cut into 1 $^1/_2$ in (4 cm) long strips
$^1/_2$ cup Korean watercress (minari)
$^1/_2$ cup sliced Chinese chives
2 medium-sized carrots, julienned
4 chestnuts, boiled, peeled and julienned

1. Cut 3 of the radishes in half lengthwise (reserve one for the stuffing). Make 3–4 deep notches lengthwise on the rounded sides of each radish half.
2. To make the brine, dissolve 6 oz (170 g) salt in the water. Soak the radish halves in the brine for about 14–16 hours or overnight. Cover the container with a saucer to completely immerse the radish. Drain and rinse under cold water. Drain again.
3. To make the stuffing, finely julienne the remaining radishes. Put the porridge, fish sauce, chili powder and flakes, chili threads, garlic, and ginger in a bowl and mix together. Add the julienned radish, scallions, minari, chives, carrots, chestnuts and gently toss all the ingredients together.
4. Insert about 1 tablespoon stuffing into each slit in the radishes. Place the radishes on their

side in the container. Rinse out the mixing bowl with $^1/_2$ cup water and the remaining salt, and pour over. Cover tightly and ferment for 3–4 weeks in the crisper section of the refrigerator.
5. To serve, cut each radish half into cubes or rectangles so that each piece will contain one stuffed notch.

Note: In the past, this kimchee was prepared in the coastal areas where pine nuts, dates, and chestnuts were uncommon. In their place, fishermen used cod or pollack chunks, which were easily available and cheap. Sometimes a whole fish fillet was fermented between 2 stuffed radish halves. The fish slabs were served separately from the radish and seasoned with sesame seeds, oil, and chopped scallions and sprinkled with red chili powder.

SPRING KIMCHEE RECIPES

These recipes make use of spring bounty such as young vine leaves, bamboo shoots, burdock and fresh watercress as they find their way to the markets. The turn is towards a slightly milder kimchee (which are no less flavoursome). Most spring kimchees go well as a condiment with meat or seafood dishes.

ALL SEASON JUICY KIMCHEE
NABAK KIMCHI
(From previous page)

This is an easily assembled all-season kimchee, but popular in the spring. It is fresh and clean-tasting if left unfermented. If fresh red chilies are not available, use red hot chili powder.

3 radishes, 3 lb (1.5 kg), cut into 1 in (2.5 cm) slices
1 Napa cabbage, 2 lb (1 kg), cut into 1 1/2 in (4 cm) pieces
1 cup Korean watercress (*minari*), cut into 2 in (5 cm) lengths
8 scallions, cut into 2 in (5 cm) lengths
1/3 cup crushed garlic
1/4 cup chopped fresh ginger
1/2 cup red hot fresh chili pepper
4 oz (115 g) coarse sea salt
1 1/2 quantities rice porridge (page 41)
1 quart (1.25 liters) water

1. Place the radish and cabbage in a container. Add the *minari* and scallions.
2. Blend the garlic, ginger and chili in a food processor. Mix with the salt, porridge and water. Pour this into the container, and mix well. You can eat immediately or allow the kimchee to sit for 1–2 days.

Note: The kimchee should be eaten within a week; otherwise it turns too sour.

STUFFED CRAB SHELL KIMCHEE
KYE SSAM KIMCHI

This is a gourmet kimchee that makes use of cleaned crab shells for presentation purposes.

12–15 large fresh crab
5 oz (140 g) coarse sea salt
1 Napa cabbage, about 2 lb (1 kg), cut into 1 1/2 in (4 cm) pieces
1 radish, about 1 lb (500 g), julienned
1/3 cup crushed garlic
1/4 cup crushed fresh ginger
3 oz (85 g) red hot chili powder
1 oz (30 g) red hot chili flakes
1/2 cup fish sauce
4 scallions, cut into 2 in (5 cm) lengths
1/2 cup Korean watercress (*minari*), cut into 2 in (5 cm) lengths

1. Rinse the crabs well, pull off the top shells, and reserve. Remove the roe and set aside. Crack open the crab legs, remove the meat. Mix the roe and meat together with 2 oz (60 g) salt. Blanch the top shells briefly in boiling water until the shells turn red, then dry thoroughly.
2. Toss the cabbage and radish with 3 oz (85 g) salt and allow to stand.
3. To make the stuffing, mix together the garlic, ginger, chili powder and flakes, and fish sauce. Add the scallions and *minari*, and toss together. Add the cabbage and radish and mix well.
4. Stuff the crab shells generously. Pile them neatly in a container with the stuffing facing up. Cover with several cabbage leaves and allow to ferment for 2–3 days. Serve the kimchee in the crab shells.

SPRING BELLFLOWER ROOT KIMCHEE
HAET TORAJI KIMCHI

Toraji (Platycodon glaucum) is a wild Korean plant found in mountainous areas. This recipe is included as an example of a traditional kimchee; the bellflower root is virtually impossible to get outside Korea, and there is no similar plant that could act as a substitute. It may, however, be cultivated by planting the roots or seeds.

6 lb (3 kg) bellflower roots, well-washed, torn into strips by hand
5 oz (140 g) salt
1 radish, 1 lb (500 g), julienned, or
1 cucumber, cut into 2 in (5 cm) lengths, ¼ in (8 mm) thick
3 oz (85 g) chopped garlic
1 oz (30 g) chopped ginger
1 oz (30 g) red hot chili flakes
3 oz (85 g) red chili powder
2 oz (60 g) sugar
4 oz (115 g) scallions, cut into 2 in (5 cm) strips

1. Mix together the roots with 3 oz (85 g) salt. Then add the radish or cucumber and toss together. Set aside for 20 minutes to allow the vegetables to wilt. Drain and reserve the liquid.
2. To make the seasoning, mix together the garlic, ginger, chili flakes and powder, sugar, and the remaining 2 oz (60 g) salt. Add to the roots and radish, then add the scallions. Put everything into a container and pour over the reserved liquid. Ferment for 2–3 days. The kimchee can be served immediately with a dash of vinegar for the fresher, strong taste of the root.

WILD LANCEOLATE ROOT KIMCHEE
TODOK KIMCHI

A mid-spring delicacy in Korea. The plant *Dodonopsis lanceolate* grows wild in North Korean mountain areas. It is a bitter root of tough fibers, similar to ginseng. When dug up in the spring, the roots are more tender and less bitter than those collected in the autumn. They are preserved by making this kimchee or are dried for use in other dishes.

6 lb (3 kg) fresh lanceolate roots
5 oz (140 g) salt
1 quantity rice porridge (page 41)
3 oz (85 g) chopped garlic
2 oz (60 g) chopped ginger
1 oz (30 g) red hot chili flakes
3 oz (85 g) red chili powder
2 oz (60 g) sugar
1 radish, 1 lb (500 g), cut into 2 in (5 cm)
    juliennes
4 oz (115 g) scallions, cut into 2 in (5 cm) strips
1 oz (30 g) pine nuts or chestnut slices

1. Clean the roots well and cut them into 2 in (5 cm) lengths. The thick part of the root should be cut to pencil thickness. Rub with 3 oz (85 g) salt to wilt for 30 minutes.
2. To make the seasoning, combine the rice porridge, garlic, ginger, chili flakes, and powder. Add the sugar and the remaining 2 oz (60 g) salt.
3. Drain and reserve the root-soaking liquid. Mix together the radish, scallions, roots and pine nuts and gradually incorporate into the seasoning mixture. Place everything into a container and pour the root liquid over it. The pickle can be served immediately with a dash of vinegar and sesame oil, or it may be fermented for 2–3 days.

YOUNG WHOLE GARLIC PICKLE
T'ONG MANUL CHORIM

This pickle has been a traditional condiment in Korea for generations and is served with meat or seafood dishes. Its delicious, nutty garlic flavour is very appealing. Choose fresh, young garlic heads, preferably with some of their green leaves attached.

5 lb (2.5 kg) whole garlic, not peeled and
    with the leaves attached
1 pint (500 ml) light soy sauce
1 quart (1.25 liters) boiling water
1/2 cup white vinegar
1/2 cup sugar

1. Trim the roots from the garlic heads as well as any wilted or brown leaves. Take one or two heads of garlic and wrap them up in a bundle by rolling the long leaves around and tying them. Place the bundles neatly and tightly in a dry container. Cover with extra garlic leaves. Press down the bundles with a plate or saucer.
2. Mix the soy sauce, water, vinegar, and sugar together; bring to a boil; and pour this over the garlic bundles.
3. Ferment for 4–6 weeks in a cool space.
To serve, cut the green leaves into 2 in- (5 cm)-long pieces. Then slice the garlic head horizontally. Serve the leaves, garlic and pickling sauce in a bowl.

MULBERRY LEAF PICKLE
PPONGNIP CHORIM

Mulberry leaves from young trees are used to feed silkworms. This pickle is prepared by collecting the late spring to early summer leaves which are bright green and tender.

6 lb (3 kg) young and tender mulberry leaves
2 gallons (8 quarts) water
7 oz (200 g) coarse sea salt
¾ quantity rice porridge (page 41)

3 oz (85 g) fish sauce
3 oz (85 g) red hot chili flakes
2 oz (60 g) chopped garlic
1 oz (30 g) chopped ginger
8 oz (230 g) scallions, tied together
   3 or 4 to a bundle

1. Tie the mulberry leaves into 20–30 leaf bundles. Prepare a brine with 2 gallons water and 3 oz (85 g) salt. Rinse the bundles briefly in the brine and drain.
2. To make the seasoning, mix together the rice porridge, fish sauce, chili, garlic, ginger, and 2 oz (60 g) salt. Hold the leaf bundles by the tied ends and dip them firmly into the seasoning. Place them flat into the container. Cover with the scallion bundles. Pour over 2 cups of water and the remaining 2 oz (60 g) salt. Press down with a heavy plate or some weights.
3. This pickle keeps for only a short period: ferment for less than a week, then refrigerate if not using immediately. The leaves are used as a wrapper for rice, or as a side dish.

SEMI-DRIED RADISH CHIPS
MU MALLAENGI CHORIM

In Korea, radishes are harvested from the end of October to November. The radishes are cut into 2 in (5 cm) pieces of pencil thickness. They are semi-dried on straw mats in the shade to maintain the white color. They are then lightly wilted by salting, squeezed to remove any extra moisture, then spread on straw mats to dry. Since huge quantities are grown, the radishes are wrapped in rice straw and buried in the ground for storage.

6 lb (3 kg) semi-dried radish strips
2 lb (1 kg) semi-dried chili leaves
1/2 lb (250 g) semi-dried radish stems
8 fl oz (230 ml) light soy sauce
1 oz (30 g) sugar
3 oz (85 g) chopped garlic
2 oz (60 g) chopped ginger
1 oz (30 g) red hot chili flakes
2 oz (60 g) red chili powder
4 oz (115 g) scallions, cut into 2 in (5 cm) lengths
1 oz (30 g) red dry chili threads
1 oz (30 g) toasted sesame seeds

1. Rinse the radish strips, chili leaves, and radish stems quickly so that they do not absorb water. Squeeze out the excess moisture gently. Mix the vegetables together. Soak them in the soy sauce and sugar overnight. Weight down the mixture with a plate.
2. To make the seasoning, combine the garlic, ginger, chili flakes and powder. Toss this with the vegetables, scallions, chili threads, and sesame seeds.
3. Transfer everything to a container and allow to sit in a cool, dark place to ferment. This pickle can be kept for many months. If you wish to eat it immediately, sprinkle the pickle with sesame oil and a little sugar (optional) or vinegar.

KOREAN WATERCRESS JUICY KIMCHEE
MINARI KIMCHI

Minari is not the same as the watercress sold in Western supermarkets, although both are grown in water. Watercress is not a perfect substitute, but will have to suffice unless you have a very enthusiastic grocer! Choose firm, thin stems.

2 lb (1 kg) Korean watercress (*minari*)
1/3 cup crushed garlic
1/4 cup crushed fresh ginger
3 oz (85 g) red hot fresh chili
2 quantities rice porridge (page 41)
5 oz (140 g) coarse sea salt
1 quart (1.25 liters) water
2 radishes, 2 lb (1 kg), cut into matchsticks
1 Napa cabbage, about 1 lb (500 g),
    cut into 1 1/2 in (4 cm) pieces
4 scallions, cut into 2 in (5 cm) lengths

1. Rinse the watercress well and drain. Pull off and use the leaves in another dish, reserving only the stems.
2. Blend the garlic, ginger, and chili in a food processor into a smooth paste. Mix with the porridge, salt, and water.
3. Place the watercress, radish, cabbage, and scallions in a container and pour over the spice mixture. This kimchee can be eaten straight away. It should not be fermented longer than 2–3 days and should be eaten within a week.

CHINESE CHIVES WITH ANCHOVY PASTE
PUCH'U CHOT KIMCHI

Use Chinese chives (*Alium tuberosum*), those with flat, dark-green leaves. This is a strongly flavored and spicy kimchee, with the pungency of anchovy paste. It is often served with squid and other greasy dishes.

5 lb (2.5 kg) Chinese chives, halved horizontally or left whole
2 radishes, 2 lb (1 kg), halved and thinly sliced
4 oz (115 g) coarse sea salt
1 quantity rice porridge (page 41)
5 oz (140 g) anchovy paste
3 oz (85 g) chopped garlic
2 oz (60 g) chopped ginger
3 oz (85 g) red hot chili flakes
2 oz (60 g) chili powder
4 oz (115 g) fresh green chilies, whole
4 oz (115 g) scallions, whole

1. Trim, rinse, and drain the chives.
2. Toss the radish slices with 3 oz (85 g) salt. Set aside for 30 mins. Drain and reserve the liquid.
3. Toss the chives with the reserved radish brine to wilt them. This creates a better surface to absorb the seasoning flavors.
4. To make the seasoning, mix together the rice porridge, anchovy paste, garlic, ginger, chili flakes and powder. Toss this with the radish.
5. Gently toss together the chives, radish, green chilies, scallions, and all the other ingredients. Place the mixture in a container, cover, and allow to ferment for 2–3 days in the refrigerator. Serve as a side dish. Refrigerate for up to 1 week.

HOT SPICY SPRING KIMCHEE
T'ONG PAECH'U POM KIMCHI

This spring kimchee is a specialty of southwest Korea, where the preference is for more salty and spicy food. The kimchee is flaming red, and very pungent.

2 large Napa cabbages, about 7 lb (3.5 kg)
8 oz (230 g) coarse sea salt
1 gallon (5 liters) water
4 oz (115 g) fermented whole anchovies
1/3 cup red hot chili flakes
1/3 cup red chili powder
2/3 cup well-crushed garlic
1/2 cup well-crushed ginger
8 scallions, cut into 1 1/2 in (4 cm) pieces
1 cup Indian mustard leaves,
    cut into 1 1/2 in (4 cm) strips
1/2 cup fish sauce

1. Trim and discard the discolored outer leaves of the cabbage. Reserve a few of the larger leaves. Cut the cabbage in half lengthwise from the top down 1/3 of the length toward the root end. Hold both parts of the cabbage firmly and pull it in half. Repeat the process with the remaining cabbage.
2. To make the brine, dissolve 7 oz (200 g) salt in the water. Soak the cabbage halves and leaves in the brine for 16–18 hours. Cover the container with a saucer to immerse the vegetables. Drain and rinse under cold water. Drain again.
3. To make the stuffing, in a large mixing bowl combine the anchovy, chili flakes, chili powder, garlic and ginger, and mix gently. Add the scallions and mustard leaves, and toss the mixture together. Add the rest of the salt. The mixture will be red.
4. Tuck the stuffing between layers of cabbage leaves. Put the halves in a container and cover with the loose cabbage leaves. Pour over the fish sauce. Cover, and ferment the kimchee for 3–4 weeks in the crisper section of the fridge.

YOUNG SPRING SCALLIONS KIMCHEE

TCHOKP'A JOT KIMCHI

Use slender, young scallions for this dish. It is a salty, spicy but refreshing, green side dish.

1 quantity rice porridge (page 41)
4 oz (115 g) fermented shrimp paste or sauce
3 oz (85 g) chopped garlic
2 oz (60 g) chopped ginger
3 oz (85 g) red hot chili flakes
2 oz (60 g) chili powder
4 oz (115 g) coarse sea salt
6 lb (3 kg) fresh young scallions (spring onions), trimmed and left whole
$1/2$ lb (250 g) carrot, julienned thinly
$1/2$ lb (250 g) onion, thinly sliced
4 oz (115 g) fresh red chili, halved lengthwise or used whole

1. To make the seasoning, combine the rice porridge, shrimp paste, garlic, ginger, chili flakes and powder, and salt.
2. Toss together the scallions, carrot, onion and fresh red chili. Mix these gently into the seasoning paste. Place everything in a container, cover and refrigerate for about 1–2 hours for the flavors to infuse. Serve immediately to taste the fresh garden flavor. If desired, this kimchee may be fermented for 2–3 days.

KITEFISH PICKLE
HONGO SOKPAKCHI

The kitefish, appropriately named, is semi-transparent and may be available cleaned and frozen from a good Asian grocer. If not, use skate or monkfish. This fish dish is commonly prepared as *Hoe* (raw fish fillet) and served with a Japanese horseradish.

5 lb (2.5 kg) kitefish, very thinly sliced
2 oz (60 g) sugar
2 cups white distilled vinegar
3 oz (85 g) red hot chili powder
1 oz (30 g) red hot chili flakes
2 radishes, 2 lb (1 kg), cut into 2 in (5 cm) strips
3 oz (85 g) salt
2 oz (60 g) fish sauce
3 oz (85 g) chopped garlic
3 oz (85 g) chopped ginger
4 oz (115 g) Korean watercress (*minari*),
    cut into 2 in (5 cm) lengths
4 oz (115 g) scallions, cut into 2 in (5 cm)
    lengths
2 oz (60 g) chestnuts, boiled, peeled and sliced

1. Slice the fish while it is still frozen to obtain paper-thin slices. Add 1 oz (30 g) sugar and the vinegar to cover the fish. Weight this down with a plate and soak overnight. The next day, drain and lightly squeeze out the liquid. Rub the fish with chili powder and flakes.
2. Toss the radish with 2 oz (60 g) salt, and allow to stand for 30 minutes to wilt. Lightly squeeze the mixture to remove any excess water. Add this to the fish and toss together.
3. Add the fish sauce, garlic, ginger, 1 oz (30 g) salt, 1 oz (30 g) sugar, *minari*, scallions, and chestnuts. Toss together gently, transfer to a covered container and store in a cool place (or the crisper section of the refrigerator) for 1–2 days. Alternatively, it may be eaten immediately if desired, with a dash of vinegar.

BURDOCK ROOT KIMCHEE
UONG KIMCHI

The burdock (*Arctium lapya*) is a strong-fibered perennial plant, available fresh and frozen from Japanese and other Asian food stores. This pickle can be served with meat, poultry or fish dishes.

6 lb (3 kg) fresh burdock root
½ quantity rice porridge (page 41)
3 oz (85 g) chopped garlic
1 oz (30 g) chopped ginger
2 oz (60 g) sugar
5 oz (140 g) salt
2 oz (60 g) red chilies, halved
1 radish, 1 lb (500 g), cut into 2 in (5 cm) strips
4 oz (115 g) scallions, cut into 2 in (5 cm) strips
1 oz (30 g) red chili threads (optional)

1. Peel the burdock and cut into 2–3 in (5–7.5 cm) lengths of pencil thickness. Soak them in cold water as you go to prevent discoloration.
2. To make the seasoning, mix together the rice porridge, garlic, ginger, sugar, and salt. Drain the burdock, rinse again with cold water, and toss with the seasoning and chili halves.
3. Add the radish, scallions, and chili threads, if used.
4. Put everything into a container, cover and ferment for 4–5 days in a cool place or the crisper section of your refrigerator.

BAMBOO SHOOTS PICKLE
CHUKSUN CHORIM

Bamboo shoots are grown mainly in the central and southern parts of Korea, and the shoots are highly prized. If you cannot find the fresh shoots in your Asian grocer, use the canned variety, but drain and boil them for 10 minutes in water to remove any metallic flavor. Serve this mellow pickle as a side dish.

5 lb (2.5 kg) fresh young tender bamboo shoots, peeled
5 oz (140 g) coarse sea salt
2 quarts (2.5 liters) water
2 lb (1 kg) light soy sauce

1. Blanch the whole, peeled, trimmed bamboo shoots in boiling water for 1 minute. Drain. Place them neatly in a dry container.
2. To prepare a colorless pickle, dissolve the salt in the water and bring to a boil. Pour it over the shoots. Cover and weight down with a plate. (Bamboo shoots prepared in this manner are used as one of the ingredients in preparing other dishes.)
3. To prepare a colored pickle, bring the soy sauce to a boil and pour it over the shoots. Cover and weight down with a plate and allow to ferment for 4–6 weeks.

SUMMER KIMCHEE RECIPES

Soupier, lighter and crunchier kimchees . . . it must be summer! The dishes here are less fermented than those in autumn and winter, and are ideal to serve as side salads to main courses or with cold noodles. Highlights of the season include the glorious lotus root, cucumber, young grape leaves, and perilla leaves.

FRESH GINSENG KIMCHEE
SUSAM NABAK KIMCHI
(From previous page)

This is a seasonal specialty kimchee – special, uncommon and expensive. Ginseng, considered a pharmaceutical plant, is cultivated and sold under a government monopoly in Korea. Fresh ginseng is impossible to find outside of Korea. It is available dried or bottled from some Asian grocers or from Chinese medicine shops, but is expensive. Use the bottled for this recipe.

2 lb (1 kg) fresh ginseng, split and cut into 2 in (5 cm) lengths
2 radish, 2 lb (1 kg), thinly sliced and cut into 2 in (5 cm) lengths
2 cucumbers, 1 lb (500 g), thinly sliced and cut into 2 in (5 cm) lengths
1/2 lb (250 g) carrot, thinly sliced and cut into thin 2 in (5 cm) lengths
2 oz (60 g) shredded ginger
1 oz (30 g) sugar
4 oz (115 g) salt
1 oz (30 g) white vinegar
5 cups water

1. Rinse the ginseng in water until thoroughly clean. Drain and place in a container. Add the radish, cucumber and carrot.
2. Top with the ginger, sugar, salt, and vinegar. Pour over the water, and stand for 1 day in a cool place (or in the refrigerator) before serving.

YOUNG SUMMER RADISH WATERY KIMCHEE
YOLMU KIMCHI

This kimchee uses the leaves of another special type of radish (*yolmu*), which grows to pencil-size (about 4 in/10 cm long) and has thick, solid, above-ground stems and leaves. It is hard to find the leafy radish outside of Korea, so substitute with watercress – it gives a completely different taste, but is tangy all the same. Serve the vegetables and liquid together as a refreshing summer side dish.

5 lb (2.5 kg) young leafy summer radish (*yolmu*) with stems and leaves
7 oz (200 g) coarse sea salt
1 gallon (5 liters) water
1/3 cup thinly sliced garlic
1/4 cup thinly sliced ginger
2–3 red hot chilies
2 quantities rice porridge (page 41)
3–4 green hot chilies
2 cups scallions, cut into 3 in (7.5 cm) lengths

1. Clean, trim and rinse the radish well. Slice into 3 in (7.5 cm) lengths. To make the brine, dissolve 5 oz (140 g) salt in 3 quarts (3 liters) water. Soak the radish pieces, stems and leaves in the brine for 2 hours. Drain, rinse in cold water, and drain again.
2. Blend the garlic, ginger, half of the red chilies and the porridge in a food processor.
3. Thinly slice the green chilies and the remaining red chilies. Combine the sliced chili, scallions, and radish in a large bowl. Pour the sauce over the vegetables and put everything into a container. Mix together the remaining 2 oz (60 g) salt and 1 quart (1.25 liters) water; rinse out the mixing bowl and pour the mixture into the container. Cover, place in a cool spot, and lightly ferment for 1–2 days.

PERILLA LEAF ROLLS
KKAENNIP MARI KIMCHI

The Chinese have their egg rolls, the Middle East its stuffed vine leaves, and the Koreans their stuffed perilla rolls. A nice, bitey kimchee.

1 lb (500 g) fresh perilla leaves
3 oz (85 g) salt
4 radish, thinly sliced and julienned
2 oz (60 g) chopped garlic
1 oz (30 g) chopped ginger
3 oz (85 g) red chili powder
4 oz (115 g) fish sauce
1/2 quantity rice porridge (page 41)
4 oz (115 g) Korean watercress (minari),
    cut into 2 in (5 cm) lengths
4 oz (115 g) Indian mustard leaves,
    cut into 2 in (5 cm) strips
4 oz (115 g) scallions, split lengthwise
    and cut into 2 in (5 cm) strips
4 oz (115 g) Chinese leek,
    cut into 2 in (5 cm) lengths
8 oz (230 g) onions, thinly sliced
1 oz (30 g) chestnuts, peeled and sliced
1 oz (30 g) red chili threads (optional)

1. Rinse the leaves and sprinkle over 1 oz (30 g) salt. Stand for 30 minutes to wilt.
2. Toss the radish with 2 oz (60 g) salt. Stand for 30 minutes.
3. To make the seasoning, mix together the garlic, ginger, chili powder, fish sauce, and rice porridge.
4. To make the stuffing, toss together with the radish, watercress, Indian mustard, scallion, leek, and onions
5. Take 1 tablespoon of the stuffing and place it on the wide part of the leaf and roll up to a cigar-like shape. Repeat with the rest of the filling and leaves. Put the rolls in a container, and press down with a plate. Cover and allow to stand for at least 1 hour. The rolls can be served immediately, as a side dish with sauce.

SOY BEAN LEAF KIMCHEE
P'UT K'ONGNIP KIMCHI

Soy bean leaves are only very rarely available outside of Korea. You can use vine leaves, perilla leaves or betel leaves in place of the soy bean for an inauthentic recipe that is none the less pungent and hot.

6 lb (3 kg) young soy bean leaves or perilla
    leaves or betel leaves
2 gallons (5 liters) water
7 oz (200 g) coarse sea salt
1 quantity rice porridge (page 41)
4 oz (115 g) fish sauce
2 oz (60 g) red hot chili flakes
1 oz (30 g) red chili powder
3 oz (85 g) chopped garlic
1 oz (30 g) chopped ginger
3 oz (85 g) scallions, thinly sliced diagonally
1 oz (30 g) chili threads (optional)

1. Clean the young, tender, unblemished leaves, and tie them into 20–30 leaf lots by the stems with cotton or hemp thread.
2. Prepare a brine with the water and 3 oz (85 g) salt. Rinse the bundles briefly in the brine and drain.
3. To make the seasoning, mix together the rice porridge, fish sauce, chili flakes and powder, garlic, ginger, and 2 oz (60 g) salt. Add the scallions and chili threads, if used.
4. Hold the bundles by the tied stems and dip them firmly into the paste to coat. Place them flat in a container. Sprinkle over the remaining 2 oz (60 g) salt, and press down with a heavy plate. Cover, and ferment for 2–3 days or longer if you want a stronger flavour.

STUFFED GREEN TOMATO KIMCHEE
TOMATO SOBAEGI

Tomatoes were introduced into Korea by Australian missionaries about 70 years ago. This tomato side dish is not common, and is an urban rather than a farmhouse kimchee. Choose firm, hard tomatoes.

5 lb (2.5 kg) green tomatoes
3 oz (85 g) chopped garlic
1 oz (30 g) chopped ginger
2 oz (60 g) red hot chili power
1 radish, 1 lb (500 g), thinly sliced and
    julienned
1 carrot, 4 oz (115 g), thinly sliced and
    julienned
2 oz (60 g) chestnuts or water chestnuts,
    peeled, boiled and thinly sliced and
    julienned
4 scallions, cut into thin strips
2 oz (60 g) coarse sea salt
1/4 cup chili threads
1 cup water
1/2 cup sugar

1. Cut the tomatoes into quarters from the top almost to the stem end. Do not cut through the stem.
2. To make the stuffing, combine the garlic, ginger, and chili; then add the radish, carrot, scallions, chestnuts and salt. Mix together gently but thoroughly.
3. Take 1 tablespoon stuffing, open the tomato quarters slightly and stuff. Place the tomatoes, stem-side down, in the container so that the stuffing does not fall out. Rinse out the mixing bowl with 1–2 cups water and pour over just enough liquid to cover. Cover, and ferment for 1–2 days in a cool place. Serve immediately if you wish, or allow to ferment a little longer to add another dimension to the flavor.

STUFFED CUCUMBER KIMCHEE
OI SOBAEGI

A cool, crunchy, juicy delicatessen-style pickle, and a popular summer kimchee. It can be eaten 24 hours after preparation. Since it turns sour quite quickly, refrigerate to prevent further fermentation.

6 lb (3 kg) young cucumbers,
    3–4 in (7.5–10 cm) long
5 oz (140 g) coarse sea salt
1/2 cup chopped garlic
1/4 cup chopped ginger
1/2 cup fermented baby shrimp paste,
    chopped
2 quantities rice porridge (page 41)
2 oz (60 g) red chili powder
1 oz (30 g) red hot chili flakes
6 scallions, very finely sliced
1/2 cup Chinese leek, thinly sliced
1 tsp sugar
1/2 cup fresh chestnuts, boiled, peeled and
    thinly julienned
1/4 cup chili threads (optional)
1 cup (250 ml) water

1. Rinse the cucumber in cold water, do not peel or trim. Drain. Rub the skins with 1 oz (30 g) salt. Set aside.
2. In each cucumber, make a 2 in (5 cm) incision almost all the way through to the other side. Turn each cucumber halfway and make another incision on the side almost to the other side. The cucumber should remain intact.
3. Sprinkle the slits with 1 oz (30 g) salt for 1 1/2 hours to soften the cucumber and to make stuffing it easier. Rinse with cold water, drain and gently squeeze to eliminate excess liquid.
4. To make the stuffing, mix the garlic, ginger, and shrimp paste in the rice porridge. Add the chili powder and flakes, and mix into a red paste. Add the scallions, leek, the remaining salt, sugar, and chestnuts, if used. Mix gently so as not to bruise the greens.
5. Take about 1 tablespoon stuffing and use to fill each cucumber. When all the cucumbers are stuffed, place them in the container. Rinse the stuffing bowl with the water and pour it over the cucumber, cover, and let them mature for 24 hours in a cool place. To serve, cut the cucumber in half. Serve at room temperature. Store any leftovers in the refrigerator for up to 1 week.

STUFFED EGGPLANT KIMCHEE
KAJI SOBAEGI

The slender Asian eggplant is chewy rather than having the crunch of a cucumber. The stuffing of carrot, radish, and scallions provides additional texture to this popular kimchee.

5 lb (2.5 kg) slender eggplant
5 oz (140 g) coarse sea salt
$1/2$ cup chopped garlic
$1/4$ cup fresh chopped ginger
$1/2$ cup fish sauce, fermented anchovy, or shrimp extract
2 oz (60 g) red chili powder
2 quantities rice porridge (page 41)
2 carrots, 1 lb (500 g), very thinly julienned
1 radish, 1 lb (500 g), very thinly julienned
6 scallions, very thinly julienned
1 tsp sugar

1. Rinse the eggplant in cold water (do not peel or trim). Make a 2 in (5 cm) incision almost all the way through from one side to another, keeping the eggplant whole. Do the same with all the eggplant. Turn halfway and make another incision on the side. Sprinkle the slits with 2 oz (60 g) salt and let stand for 1 $1/2$ hours to wilt. Then rinse with cold water, drain, and gently squeeze to eliminate any excess liquid. The eggplants are now ready to stuff.
2. To make the stuffing, combine the garlic, ginger, fish sauce, and chili with the porridge. Add the carrot, radish, scallion, 3 oz (85 g) salt, and sugar. Mix everything together gently.
3. Gently open the incisions in the eggplant and stuff with 1 tablespoon of stuffing.
4. Stack the stuffed eggplant container and sprinkle over the excess stuffing. Press the eggplant down with a heavy plate, cover and let the kimchee ferment in a cool spot for 2 days, during which liquid will accumulate. To serve, cut the eggplant into 4 in (10 cm) lengths. Refrigerate any leftover kimchee.

GREEN HARD PERSIMMON KIMCHEE
P'UT KAM KIMCHI

This is a traditional Korean pickle that is made in the summer, and served as a fruit snack during the cold winter months (after a period of 3–4 months of fermentation). Use small (2–3 in/5–7.5 cm diameter), hard, green persimmons, and keep the sepals on. The cinnamon adds a distinctive flavour. The alum is added to prevent discoloring, not for flavor.

6 lb (3 kg) fresh green hard persimmons
3 oz (85 g) salt

3 cups boiling water
2 oz (60 g) cinnamon stick (optional)
$1/2$ tsp alum

1. Select unblemished fruit. Wipe with a dry towel – do not rinse. Put the fruit gently into a container (traditionally an earthenware jar is used) and weight down with a plate or stone.
2. Prepare a brine with the salt and boiling water. Pour into the container with the cinnamon stick (if used) and the alum.
3. Ferment for 3–4 months to reduce the tannin in the fruit. The persimmon sweetens during the fermentation; the result is a delicious snack.

SAVOY CABBAGE KIMCHEE
YANG PAECH'U MAK KIMCHI

Savoy cabbage is a wrinkly-leaf variety of cabbage, with a milder flavor than its hard-balled, smooth-leafed cousin. This is a very flavorsome and mellow kimchee that can be served with anything. It is sometimes served as a garnish on top of Korea's famous cold noodles.

13/14 quarts (2–2.5 liters) water
7 oz (200 g) coarse sea salt
2 cucumbers, 1 lb (500 g)
4 lb (2 kg) Savoy cabbage, cut into
　　1 in (2.5 cm) pieces
2 quantities rice porridge (page 41)
2/3 cup fish sauce
1/2 cup chopped garlic
1/3 cup chopped ginger
1/3 cup red hot chili flakes
1 oz (30 g) sugar
1 cup thinly sliced and julienned carrot
1 cup thinly julienned scallions

1. Mix together 5–6 cups water and 5 oz (140 g) salt to make a brine. Soak the whole cucumbers and sliced cabbage in the brine overnight, about 12–14 hours. Drain and rinse the vegetables lightly with cold water.
2. To make the seasoning, mix together the rice porridge, fish sauce, garlic, ginger, chili, and sugar. Add the carrot, scallion, and cabbage. At this stage, cut the wilted cucumbers in half lengthwise, then each half into 3 equal parts. Mix these into the seasoning.
3. Place all the mixture into a container, sprinkle with the remaining 2 oz (60 g) salt, and add the remaining water. Ferment for 1–2 days in a cool place.

YOUNG GREEN LEAFY SUMMER CABBAGE KIMCHEE

P'UT PAECH'U KIMCHI

This Korean cabbage is more like long-leafed lettuce. You can use a soft lettuce such as cos (romaine) or even baby *bok choy* in place of the cabbage. You can serve this kimchee as a spiced salad. It is ideal with roasted or grilled meats.

7 lb (3.5 kg) summer cabbage, cut into
    3–4 in (7.5–10 cm) lengths
8 oz (230 g) coarse sea salt
1 gallon (5 liters) water
$1/3$ cup thinly sliced garlic
$1/4$ cup thinly sliced fresh ginger
$2/3$ cup fish paste, fermented anchovy
    or shrimp
$1/3$ cup red hot chili flakes
$1/4$ cup red chili powder
10 scallions, cut into 3 in (7.5 cm) lengths

1. Clean and trim the cabbage. Dissolve 5 oz (140 g) salt in 1 gallon (5 liters) water to make the brine. Soak the cabbage in the brine for 2 hours to wilt. Drain, rinse in cold water, and drain again.
2. Blend the garlic, ginger, fish paste, chili flakes and powder together in a food processor. Mix this red paste gently with the cabbage and scallions. Put everything into a container. Sprinkle the remaining salt over the top.

PERILLA KIMCHEE
KKAENNIP KIMCHI

Use fresh, young perilla (sesame) leaves for this appetizing summer kimchee. It can be prepared either as an instant dish, or may be kept for a long period of time.

6 lb (3 kg) young perilla (sesame) leaves, including stems
2 gallons (10 liters) water
7 oz (200 g) coarse sea salt
1 quantity rice porridge (page 41)
4 oz (115 g) fish sauce
2 oz (60 g) red hot chili flakes
1 oz (30 g) red chili powder
3 oz (85 g) chopped garlic
1 oz (30 g) chopped ginger
3 oz (85 g) scallions, thinly sliced diagonally
1 oz (30 g) chili threads (optional)

1. Tie the clean, unblemished leaves into 20–30 leaf bunches by the stems with cotton or hemp thread. Prepare a brine with the water and 3 oz (85 g) salt. Rinse the bundles briefly in the brine and drain.
2. To make the seasoning, combine the rice porridge, fish sauce, chili flakes and powder, garlic, ginger, and 2 oz (60 g) salt. Add the scallions and chili threads, if used.
3. Hold the bundles by the tied stems. Dip them firmly into the paste to season and place them flat in a container. Sprinkle over with the remaining 2 oz (60 g) salt. Weight down the ingredients with a heavy plate. If the kimchee is to be served immediately, take as many bundles as wanted and steam for 1 minute over boiling water to lightly soften. The seasoning will penetrate the leaves, which remain green. The kimchee may also be fermented for several weeks in the refrigerator in a covered container, and can be eaten over a fairly long period.

SWISS CHARD KIMCHEE
KUNDAE KIMCHEE

This is a short-term specialty prepared during the summer months. Swiss chard is also known as sliverbeet or seakale beet – use leaves and stalks for a fresh summer flavour.

1 gallon (5 liters) water
5 oz (140 g) salt
5 lb (2.5 kg) chard, whole leaf and stem
1 radish, 1 lb (500 g), julienned
3 oz (85 g) chopped garlic
2 oz (60 g) chopped ginger
4 oz (115 g) fish sauce
4 oz (115 g) rice porridge (page 41)
2 oz (60 g) red hot chili flakes
1 oz (30 g) red chili powder
1 lb (500 g) scallions, split in half lengthwise and cut into 3 in (7.5 cm) lengths
1 oz (30 g) sugar
1 oz (30 g) red chili threads

1. Prepare a light brine with the water and 2 oz (60 g) salt. Soak the chard for 30 mins. Drain.
2. Toss the radish with 1 oz (30 g) salt. Set aside.
3. To make the seasoning, combine the garlic, ginger, fish sauce, rice porridge, chili flakes and powder. Mix this with the chard, radish, and scallions. Add the sugar, the remaining 2 oz (60 g) salt, and the chili threads. Place in a container and allow to sit in a cool place for 1–2 days. You can also serve this kimchee immediately, with a dash of vinegar and sugar.

LOTUS ROOTS PICKLE
YONGUN CHORIM

Choose young, slender lotus roots for this kimchee. Serve the type seasoned in soy sauce as a side dish; it is redolent with the flavors of soy sauce, garlic and the bite of chili. The colorless pickle is used as an ingredient in stir-fry or other dishes.

5 lb (2.5 kg) lotus roots
5 oz (140 g) coarse sea salt
2 1/2 cups water
2 1/2 cups light soy sauce
2 oz (60 g) ginger
1 lb (500 g) garlic cloves, peeled
1 oz (30 g) dry, whole red chili

1. Scrub the lotus roots well and trim both ends well. Slice the lotus roots into 1/8–1/4 in (2–5 mm) thick pieces. Rinse well again. Blanch the sliced lotus root in boiling water for 1–2 minutes. Drain well and place the slices neatly in a dry container.
2. To make a colorless pickle, combine the salt and water and bring to a boil. Pour the brine over the lotus root. Press down with a plate.
3. To make a colored pickle, bring the soy sauce, ginger, garlic, and chili to a boil and pour it over the lotus root. Press down with a plate. Both pickles can be left to ferment in a cool place for 4–8 weeks.

HOT AND SPICY CUCUMBER CHUNKS
OI KKAKTUGI

The seasoning for this kimchee can be prepared in advance and stored in the fridge for up to 2 months to be used as needed. This preliminary step is a time saver, and leads to the term 'instant kimchee' or one that can be assembled at a moment's notice.

6 lb (3 kg) small cucumbers
5 oz (140 g) coarse sea salt
1 quantity rice porridge (page 41)
4 oz (115 g) fish sauce
3 oz (85 g) chopped garlic
1 oz (30 g) chopped ginger
1 oz (30 g) sugar

3 oz (85 g) red hot chili flakes
1 radish, 1 lb (500 g), thinly sliced and julienned
1 small carrot, thinly sliced and julienned
4 oz (115 g) scallions, thinly sliced

1. Trim both ends of the cucumbers, quarter, and cut into 1/2 in (4 cm) chunks. Sprinkle with 3 oz (85 g) salt and toss to mix. Set aside for 30 minutes. Drain the cucumbers and reserve the liquid.
2. To make the seasoning, combine the rice porridge, fish sauce, garlic, ginger, sugar, 2 oz (60 g) salt, and chili flakes. Add the radish, carrot, scallion, cucumber, and reserved liquid. Toss gently to mix.
3. Put everything in a container. You can serve this kimchee immediately, or refrigerate it.

CUCUMBER JUICY KIMCHEE
OI NABAK KIMCHI

A fresh kimchee that is refreshing and clean-tasting. It can be sprinkled with vinegar and sugar at serving time to enhance the fresh flavor. Some people ferment it over a long period, but this is not the original intention of the dish. Similarly, carrot was not an original ingredient in this traditional kimchee (it was devised before carrots were grown in Korea), but some people think it enhances the flavour.

3 lb (1.5 kg) small, young cucumbers, sliced
1 radish, 1 lb (500 g), julienned
½ small cabbage, 1 lb (500 g), cut into
    1 ½ in (4 cm) pieces
1 cup scallions, cut into 2 in (5 cm) pieces
⅓ cup garlic
¼ cup ginger
3 oz (85 g) red hot fresh chili
2 quantities rice porridge (page 41)
5 oz (140 g) coarse sea salt
1 quart (1.25 liters) water

1 medium-sized carrot, julienned (optional)
1. Place the cucumber, radish, cabbage, and scallions into a container.
2. Blend the garlic, ginger, and chili into a smooth paste in a food processor. Mix this with the rice porridge, salt, and water. Pour the mixture over the vegetables.
3. Cover, and shake the container lightly to mix everything together.
4. Serve immediately if you wish, or ferment for 2–3 days. The kimchee should be eaten within one week.

WRAPPED CUCUMBER KIMCHEE
OI SSAM KIMCHI

4 lb (2 kg) young slender cucumber
2 quarts (2.5 liters) water
5 oz (140 g) salt
about 30 cabbage leaves, 1 ½ lb (750 g)
2 radishes, 2 lb (1 kg), thinly sliced and
    julienned
3 oz (85 g) chopped garlic
2 oz (60 g) chopped ginger
4 oz (115 g) fermented baby shrimp paste
½ quantity rice porridge (page 41)
3 oz (85 g) red chili powder
1 oz (30 g) sugar
4 oz (115 g) scallions, split lengthwise and
    cut into 2 in (5 cm) strips
2 oz (60 g) Chinese leek, cut into
    1 in (2.5 cm) lengths
2 oz (60 g) chestnuts, peeled and sliced

1. Trim the ends of the cucumber. Cut into half
horizontally. Prepare a brine with the water and
4 oz (115 g) salt. Soak the cucumber and
cabbage leaves, pressed down with a plate,
in the brine for 1 hour to wilt them. Drain and
rinse quickly with cold water. Set aside.
2. Sprinkle the radish with 1 oz (30 g) salt and
allow to stand for 15 minutes. Drain and
reserve the liquid.
3. To make the seasoning, combine the garlic,
ginger, shrimp paste, rice porridge, chili powder
and sugar. Toss together with radish, scallions,
leek, and chestnut to make the stuffing.
4. Spread the filling on one half of the cucumber and place the other half on top. Put the
cucumber in a cabbage leaf and roll up into a
sausage shape. Repeat, until all ingredients
are used up.
5. Place the rolls in a container and pour over
the reserved radish liquid. Cover and allow to
stand for at least 30 minutes for the flavors to
infuse. Serve immediately with a dash vinegar,
or store for up to 3 days in the refrigerator.

WHOLE CUCUMBER IN BRINE
OI TCHANJI

The typical Korean cucumber is about 4–7 in (10–18 cm) long and about 1 1/2 in (4 cm) in diameter. Use young cucumber for this recipe, and keep the skins on. This crunchy, moreish pickle tastes rather like a pickled gherkin if you omit the garlic and chili. It is usually served with some far spicier kimchees.

5 lb (2.5 kg) cucumber
1 quart (1.25 liters) water
1 cup coarse sea salt
3 oz (85 g) whole garlic cloves (optional)
1 oz (30 g) red hot dry whole chili (optional)
3/4 quantity rice porridge (page 41) (optional)

1. Rinse and drain the cucumbers. Place them tightly in a dry container. Weight them down with a heavy plate.
2. Combine the water and salt, and bring to a rapid boil. Pour the hot brine over the cucumbers.
3. Store the container in a cool, dark place or in the refrigerator. For short-term preservation include the garlic, chili and rice porridge, which are added with the water. For long-term preservation omit the three optional items.
4. To serve, soak the cucumbers in cold water for 1–2 hours. Slice thinly or cut into chunks, or soak the sliced cucumbers in cold water to make a juicy (watery) kimchee.

GREEN CHILI PICKLE
P'UT KOCH'U CHORIM

Pickling green chilies was the only way that these essential items could be served out of season. For centuries, this type of preserved chili dish has been a year-round staple condiment in Korean households. These strong, spicy pickles are served as a condiment and side dish. This kimchee is customarily eaten with meat, fish, and other dishes.

6 lb (3 kg) hot, green chilies,
    2–3 in (5–7.5 cm) long, stems on
3/4 cup anchovy paste
1 cup fish sauce
3 oz (85 g) chopped garlic
2 oz (60 g) chopped ginger
3 oz (85 g) red hot chili flakes

1. Rinse the chilies well and drain. Set aside.
2. Mix together the anchovy paste, fish sauce, garlic, ginger, and chili flakes. Mix the paste with the chili and put everything into a dry container. Press down the contents with a heavy plate and cover.
3. Ferment the pickle for 1–3 months.

YOUNG GRAPE LEAF PICKLE
PODONNIP CHORIM

Grapevines were introduced into Korea by missionaries about 100 years ago. Choose young vine leaves.

6 lb (3 kg) young tender vine leaves, stems on
3/4 quantity rice porridge (page 41)
3 oz (85 g) fish sauce
2 oz (60 g) red hot chili flakes
3 oz (85 g) chopped garlic
1 oz (30 g) chopped ginger
5 oz (140 g) coarse sea salt
4 oz (115 g) scallions, thinly sliced
3–4 cabbage leaves, wilted (optional)
2 cups water

1. Rinse the vine leaves well and drain.
2. To make the seasoning, combine the rice porridge, fish sauce, chili, garlic, ginger, and 3 oz (85 g) salt. Mix in the scallions. Add the vine leaves and stems and toss the mixture.
3. Place all in a container, and cover with the cabbage leaves. Add the water and sprinkle over the rest of the salt. Press down with a heavy plate. Cover, and ferment for 2–3 days.

AUTUMN KIMCHEE RECIPES

The radish and cabbage, coupled with the other indispensables such as chilli, garlic and fish paste, really come into their own in colder month kimchees. The recipes here would have traditionally been made at harvest time, when the frosts are just settling in, and the last of the crops pulled out of the ground. The chewy texture of the kimchee and the heat from the red paste are appetite-enhancing.

FRESH OYSTERS KIMCHEE
SAENGGUL KIMCHI
(From previous page)

This is an autumn specialty, made when the shucked oysters are available. The kimchee is not fermented, but marinated.

1 gallon (5 liters) water
5 oz (140 g) salt
5 lb (2.5 kg) small to medium-sized fresh, whole oysters
2 radishes, thinly sliced and julienned
3 oz (85 g) chopped garlic
3 oz (85 g) chopped ginger
4 oz (115 g) fish sauce
3 oz (85 g) red hot chili flakes
4 oz (115 g) scallions, cut into 2 in (5 cm) strips
2 oz (60 g) chestnuts, boiled, peeled and sliced
2 oz (60 g) pine nuts (optional)
2 oz (60 g) red dry chili threads
3 oz (85 g) Korean watercress (minari) or watercress stems

1. Prepare a brine with the water and 3 oz (85 g) salt. Soak the oysters in the brine for 30 minutes. This makes the texture firm. Drain.
2. Sprinkle the radish with 1 oz (30 g) salt; toss lightly to wilt.
3. To make the seasoning, combine the garlic, ginger, fish sauce, chili flakes, and the remaining 1 oz (30 g) salt. Add the oysters, radish, scallions, watercress, chestnuts, pine nuts, if used, and chili threads. Toss gently to mix.
4. Put into a container and keep in a cool place. Serve immediately; add a dash of vinegar and toasted sesame seeds, if you wish.

FRESHLY HARVESTED AUTUMN CABBAGE KIMCHEE
KAUL PAECH'U KOTCHORI

A texturally interesting kimchee: the crunch and sweetness of the persimmon and pears are a terrific foil for the slightly chewy cabbage.

3 autumn cabbages, about 6 lb (3 kg)
5 oz (140 g) salt
3 oz (85 g) chopped garlic
2 oz (60 g) chopped ginger
4 oz (115 g) fish paste
1 oz (30 g) red hot chili flakes
2 oz (60 g) red chili powder
1 oz (30 g) sugar
8 oz (230 g) scallions, halved lengthwise, then crosswise
8 oz (230 g) Korean watercress (minari), halved crosswise
4 oz (115 g) Chinese chives, halved crosswise
1 oz (30 g) red dry chili threads
2 oz (60 g) chestnuts, boiled, peeled and sliced
4 oz (115 g) red sweet hard persimmon, julienned (optional)
5 oz (140 g) Korean pear (nashi) or Beurre Bosc pears
2 fl oz (60 ml) white vinegar

1. Split each cabbage leaf lengthwise, then cut crosswise into 1 in x 6 in (2.5 cm x 15 cm) pieces. Toss with 3 oz (85 g) salt, and allow to stand for 2 hours. Rinse and drain.
2. To make the seasoning, combine the garlic, ginger, fish paste, chili flakes and powder, sugar, and the remaining 2 oz (60 g) salt.
3. Now mix together the seasoning, cabbage, scallions, minari, chives, chili threads, chestnuts, persimmon, and vinegar. Toss well. Serve immediately as an instant kimchee.

MIXED VEGETABLE INSTANT KIMCHEE
SOKPAK KOTCHORI

Young, green, fresh summer cabbage leaves are used for this instant kimchee. For an inauthentic substitute, try cos (romaine) lettuce or whole heads of baby bok choy. This is more a hot and tangy salad than a kimchee.

5 oz (140 g) salt
3 lb (1.5 kg) leafy green cabbage, left in 5–6 in (12.5–15 cm) lengths
2 lb (1 kg) young summer radish leaves or watercress (extra, see below)
3 oz (85 g) chopped garlic
2 oz (60 g) chopped ginger
4 oz (115 g) fish paste
2 oz (60 g) red hot chili flakes
3 oz (85 g) red chili powder
1 oz (30 g) sugar
1 lb (500 g) Indian mustard leaves
1 lb (500 g) Korean watercress (minari), cut into 5–6 in (12.5–15 cm) lengths
5 oz (140 g) scallions, cut into 5–6 in (12.5–15 cm) lengths
2 oz (60 g) pine nuts (optional)
1 oz (30 g) red dry chili threads
1 oz (30 g) sesame seeds, toasted
2 oz (60 g) white vinegar

1. Sprinkle 3 oz (85 g) salt on the cabbage and radish leaves. Toss together and stand for 30 minutes. Rinse and drain.
2. To make the seasoning, combine the garlic, ginger, fish paste, chili flakes and powder, sugar and 2 oz (60 g) salt.
3. Mix the seasoning with the cabbage, radish, Indian mustard, watercress, scallions, pine nuts, chili threads, sesame seeds and vinegar. Toss together and serve as a fresh salad. Any leftover kimchee should be placed in a container and served within a few days. This is not a fermented pickle.

PONYTAIL RADISH WATERY KIMCHEE
CH'ONGGAK MU TONGCH'IMI

The radishes used in this kimchee are common in Korea: small with a pinned-in waist and long, fluttery stems and leaves, thus the description of ponytail. Normal radishes can be substituted.

7 radishes, about 7 lb (3.5 kg)
8 oz (230 g) coarse sea salt
1 gallon (5 liters) water
6–8 scallions, trimmed and left whole
10 cured green, hot chilies (page 91)
1/2 cup thinly sliced garlic
1/3 cup thinly sliced fresh ginger
1 1/2 quantities rice porridge (page 41)

1. Choose radishes with long stems and leaves. Clean well.
2. To make the brine, dissolve 5 oz (140 g) salt in 3 quarts (3.75 liters) water. Soak the radishes and scallions in the brine for 6–8 hours. Drain, rinse in cold water, and drain again thoroughly.
3. Fold the wilted radish stems around each radish back and forth lengthwise. Bury 1 or 2 cured chilies in the wrapping. Take one wilted scallion, wrap it around each radish waist and tie it neatly (you can include the chilies now if the radishes came without their greens).
4. Pile all the radishes into a container and place the garlic and ginger on top of the radish. Mix the rice porridge, the remaining 2 oz (60 g) salt, and 1 quart (1.25 liters) water, and pour over to cover the radish. Cover, and keep in a cool spot for 1–2 weeks to mature.

5. To serve, slice the radish lengthwise into 4. The stems, leaves and scallions are cut separately the same length as the radish sections. Serve with the pickling liquid.

Note: The cured green chili is also served as a condiment. Rinse the chili after it has been cured and soak it in a sweet–sour vinegar. Or season the cured chili with a spiced anchovy sauce or serve with red pepper paste (koch'ujang) or bean paste (toenjang).

HOT FISH-FLAVORED KIMCHEE
T'ONG PAECH'U CHOT KIMCHI

This is another type of whole cabbage kimchee. Long-lasting, it is served as it comes from the pickling container to the table, where it is torn into strips by hand and used to wrap around prepared meat, fish and rice. The longer it sits, the stronger the taste. The fermented fish can be omitted, but the final result will not be as fragrant.

2 large Napa cabbage
7 oz (200 g) coarse sea salt
1 gallon (5 liters) water
1 lb (500 g) scallions
1/2 lb (250 g) Chinese chives
4 fresh green hot chili, left whole
2/3 cup crushed garlic
1/3 cup crushed fresh ginger
1/3 cup red hot chili flakes
1/3 cup red chili powder
1 cup whole yellow fermented baby corvina
1/2 cup fish sauce

1. Trim and discard the discolored outer leaves of the cabbage. Cut it in half lengthwise from the top down 1/3 of the length toward the root end. Hold both parts of the cabbage firmly and pull it in half. Repeat the process with the remaining cabbage.
2. To make the brine, dissolve the salt in the water. Soak the cabbage halves in the brine overnight or for at least 16–18 hours. Cover the container with a saucer to completely immerse the vegetables. Drain and rinse under cold water. Drain again.
3. Trim the scallions but leave them whole. Rinse well and set aside. Rinse the chives in cold water and cut into 1 1/2 in (4 cm) long pieces.
4. To make the stuffing, toss together the chives and green chilies. Add the garlic, ginger, chili flakes, chili powder and the fermented fish. Toss gently and thoroughly.
5. Divide the scallions into 4 equal parts. Put one bunch on the inner cut side of the 4 cabbage halves. Tie up the bundle with 2–3 scallions. Repeat with the rest. Put the bundles into the container and pour over the fish sauce. Cover, and ferment the kimchee for 2–3 weeks in a cool place.

LIGHT AND REFRESHING FESTIVE AUTUMN WHOLE CABBAGE KIMCHEE
T'ONG PAECH'U KAUL KIMCHI

A tangy kimchee that originated in the north of the Korean peninsula. It is less spicy than usual kimchees, and the natural flavors of the cabbage are allowed to come through.

2 large Napa cabbage
2 Korean radish
6 oz (170 g) salt
1 gallon (5 liters) water
1 quantity rice porridge (page 41)
1/4 cup fish sauce
1/3 cup red hot chili flakes
1/2 cup red chili powder
1/2 cup shredded fresh garlic
1/4 cup peeled and shredded fresh ginger
4 oz (115 g) scallions, cut into 1 1/2 in (4 cm) strips
4–5 chestnuts, boiled, peeled and shredded
3 dates
2 pieces dried cloud's ear mushrooms, soaked in water and sliced
1 sweet persimmon, peeled and julienned
1 Korean pear (nashi) or Beurre Bosc pear, peeled, sliced and julienned
1 cup fresh whole oysters or 1 cup cleaned and thinly sliced squid, cut into 1 1/2 in (4 cm) lengths
1 tsp sugar (optional)
1/4 tsp MSG (optional)

1. Trim and discard the discolored outer leaves of the cabbage. Cut it in half lengthwise from the top down 1/3 of the length toward the root end. Hold both parts of the cabbage firmly and pull it in half. Repeat the process with the remaining cabbage. Trim the radish and cut in half from the tip through to the root end.
2. To make the brine, dissolve 5 oz (140 g) salt in the water. Soak the cabbage and radish halves in the brine overnight or for 16–18 hours. Cover the container with a saucer to completely immerse the vegetables. Drain and rinse under cold water. Drain again.
3. To make the stuffing, in a large mixing bowl combine the porridge, fish sauce, chili flakes, red chili powder, garlic, ginger, and scallions, and gently mix together. Then add the chestnuts, dates, mushrooms, persimmon, pear, and the oysters or squid. Toss everything together, but with a sense of neatness and orderliness. Add the remaining 1 tbs salt.
4. Distribute the stuffing between the layers of cabbage leaves, using all of it. Place one half of the radish on top of the stuffed inner leaves, like a sandwich. Take 2 outer leaves still attached to the core and wrap them around the radish to hold them together. Place in the container. Loose cabbage leaves and radish leaves can be used to cover the contents. If there is still space in the container, add 1/2–1 cup brine. Cover, and allow to ferment in a cool place for 3–4 weeks. To serve the kimchee, slice the cabbage and radish together into thin half-moon slices.

Note: There is some, but not much, fresh ginger in the kimchee because an excess amount in the fermenting mixture may produce a bitter taste.

SHREDDED RADISH WITH FRESH OYSTERS KIMCHEE
MU CH'AE KIMCHI

The white, fresh new crop of tender yet pungent autumn radishes, which are used in this kimchee, make for a feast in the harvest season. Reduce the chili flakes and powder for a milder flavor.

6 radishes, julienned
8 oz (230 g) carrots, julienned
1 lb (500 g) whole fresh oysters
5 oz (140 g) coarse sea salt
1 quantity rice porridge (page 41)
4 oz (115 g) fermented shrimp sauce
3 oz (85 g) chopped garlic
2 oz (60 g) chopped ginger
3 oz (85 g) red hot chili flakes
1 oz (30 g) red dry chili powder
1 tsp sugar
4 oz (115 g) scallions, cut into 2 in (5 cm) lengths

1. Toss the radish and carrots with 2 oz (60 g) salt. Set aside for 30 minutes. Drain and reserve the liquid.
2. Rinse the oysters in cold water, drain and mix with 3 oz (85 g) salt. Set aside for 30 minutes, then drain and reserve the liquid.
3. To make the seasoning, combine the rice porridge, shrimp sauce, garlic, ginger, chili flakes and powder, sugar and the reserved radish/carrot and oyster liquids.
4. Toss together the radish, carrot, scallions and oyster with the seasoning, and place the mixture in a container. Cover, and store in a refrigerator. You can serve the kimchee immediately as a spiced salad or ferment for 2–3 days.

SCALE-CUT RADISH KIMCHEE
PINUL MU CHOT KIMCHI

The method of cutting the radish is to imitate the rounded scales of a large fish. Select a medium-sized radish rather than the thick, bulbous type.

6 medium-sized radishes, 6 lb (3 kg), unpeeled
5 oz (140 g) coarse sea salt
1 quantity rice porridge (page 41)
5 oz (140 g) fish paste
3 oz (85 g) chopped garlic
2 oz (60 g) chopped ginger
2 oz (60 g) red hot chili flakes
3 oz (85 g) red chili powder
1 oz (30 g) sugar
3 oz (85 g) scallions, cut into
    1 1/2 in (4 cm) lengths

1. Cut the radish in half lengthwise. Then, angling your knife slightly, make diagonal cuts about 1 1/2 in (4 cm) deep at 1/2 (1 cm) intervals to simulate fish scales. Repeat with the remaining radish halves. Toss them with 3 oz (85 g) salt and stand for 30 minutes. Drain and reserve the radish liquid.
2. To make the seasoning, combine the rice porridge, fish paste, garlic, ginger, chili flakes and powder, 2 oz (60 g) salt, and sugar.
3. Toss the radish, scallions and the seasoning paste together gently. Put the mixture into a container. Rinse out mixing bowl with the radish liquid and pour into the container. Cover, and ferment for 2–3 days. Serve as a side dish.

STUFFED PONYTAIL RADISH KIMCHEE
CH'ONGGAK MU SOBAEGI

A lightly fermented kimchee that makes an ideal side dish to be served with meat or noodles. A strong-tasting, hot kimchee.

5 ponytail or ordinary radishes, 5 lb (2.5 kg)
7 oz (200 g) coarse sea salt
2 quantities rice porridge (page 41)
2/3 cup fish paste (fermented anchovy is best)
1/2 cup chopped garlic
1/3 cup chopped ginger
3 oz (85 g) red chili powder
2 oz (60 g) red hot chili flakes
1 tsp sugar
1/2 cup carrot, thinly sliced and julienned
1 cup scallions, cut into 1 1/2 in (4 cm) strips
1 cup julienned radish
1/2 cup sliced Chinese chives
1 cup water

1. Scrub and clean the radishes but do not peel. Cut off the leaves and stems and reserve. Cut the radish crossways into 4, from the stem almost to the root end.
2. Sprinkle 4 oz (115 g) salt over the radishes and any leaves and stems. Let it stand to wilt for 2–4 hours.
3. To make the stuffing, combine the rice porridge, fish paste, garlic, ginger, chili, and sugar, and mix well. Add the carrot, scallions, radish, and chives, and toss together gently.
4. Rinse and drain the radish, leaves, and stems. Take 1 tbsp of the stuffing and stuff each radish. Press the radish prongs together and place horizontally in a container. Repeat with the rest of the radish and stuffing. Tub the mixing bowl with the leaves and stems and place them over the stuffed radish. Rinse out the mixing bowl with 1 cup water, and pour in enough water to cover the radish. Sprinkle over the remaining 3 oz (85 g) salt. Weight the radish down, cover, and ferment for 2–3 days in the refrigerator.

REFRESHING CUBED RADISH KIMCHEE
PAEK KKAKTUGI

Since this kimchee is not highly seasoned or fermented, it lends itself to being served with other cuisines, Asian or Western. The refreshing kimchee is also an appetite enhancer, and is reputed to assist digestion. It does not keep for long periods; two days' fermentation is sufficient to develop the characteristic flavor.

7 radishes
5 oz (140 g) coarse sea salt
2 oz (60 g) sugar
1 tsp finely chopped fresh ginger
2 tsp finely chopped garlic
4 cups water

1. Clean the radish well and cut into 3/4 in–1 in (2–2.5 cm) cubes. Toss with the salt and stand in a large bowl. (If the radish is freshly harvested, it will contain moisture. This is sufficient to produce a liquid after salting. An older radish requires additional water to produce a liquor.)
2. Add the sugar. Squeeze the ginger and garlic together in a press and add the juice to the kimchee. Or wrap the ginger and garlic in a piece of cheesecloth and place it in the container.
3. Add the water and mix everything together. Serve the radish and liquid immediately. It can be served with a colorless vinegar. The remaining kimchee can be fermented in a cool place for 3–4 days. Vinegar is not added when fermenting.

AUTUMN PUMPKIN KIMCHEE
HOBAK KIMCHI

The Korean pumpkin (*Cucurbita moschata*) is round and smooth-surfaced, with yellow flesh. You may reduce the quantities of fermented shrimp used for a milder kimchee. The sweetness of the pumpkin is a pleasant foil for the heat and pungency of the chilies.

2 quarts (2.5 liters) water
5 oz (140 g) salt
5 lb (2.5 kg) pumpkin, peeled, seeded, and cut into 1 in (2.5 cm) slices
1 small cabbage, cut into 1 1/2 in (4 cm) lengths
8 oz (230 g) radish leaves or watercress, cut into 1 1/2 in (4 cm) lengths
3 oz (85 g) chopped garlic
2 oz (60 g) chopped ginger
2 oz (60 g) red chili powder
4 oz (115 g) fermented baby shrimp paste
4 oz (115 g) scallions, halved lengthwise and cut into 1 1/2 in (4 cm) lengths

1. Prepare a brine with the water and 2 oz (60 g) salt. Soak the pumpkin pieces in the brine for 1 hour. Drain.
2. Toss the cabbage and radish leaves or watercress with 2 oz (60 g) salt. Stand for 30 minutes to wilt. Drain and reserve the soaking liquid.
3. To make the seasoning, combine the garlic, ginger, chili powder and shrimp paste. Toss the seasoning with the pumpkin, cabbage, radish leaves and scallions.
4. Put the mixture into a container, cover with several whole cabbage leaves, and sprinkle with the remaining 1 oz (30 g) salt. Cover, and let the kimchee mature for 2–3 days before serving.

SWEET POTATO VINE PICKLE
KOGUMAJULGI KIMCHI

Another authentic recipe using a traditional Korean ingredient that might be a little hard to locate elsewhere. In Korea, the vines are collected and processed after the sweet potatoes have been harvested. Prepared vines are available, salted, dried, or frozen from some Japanese or Korean grocers. For an inauthentic substitute, try water convolvulus (*kangkung*) or young watercress stems.

6 lb (3 kg) sweet potato vines, no leaves,
    cut into 3 in (7.5 cm) pieces
5 oz (140 g) salt
1 radish, cut into 3 in lengths
3 oz (85 g) chopped garlic
2 oz (60 g) chopped ginger
4 oz (115 g) fish sauce
1 quantity rice porridge (page 41)
1 oz (30 g) red hot chili flakes
2 oz (60 g) red chili powder
6 oz (170 g) scallions, cut into
    3 in (7.5 cm) lengths
1 oz (30 g) sesame seeds, toasted (optional)

1. Crack the sweet potato vines by hand and pull out the strings as one might do with celery. Sprinkle 2 oz (60 g) salt on the fresh stems and stand for 1–2 hours to wilt. Rinse quickly and drain.
2. Sprinkle 1 oz (30 g) salt over the radish stems and stand for 30 minutes. Rinse quickly and drain.
3. To make the seasoning, combine the garlic, ginger, fish sauce, rice porridge, chili flakes and powder, and the remaining 2 oz (60 g) salt. Toss with the vines, radish, scallions, and sesame seeds. Put everything into a container, cover and allow to ferment for a few days in a cool place.

KING SCALLIONS KIMCHEE
T'ONG TAEP'A KIMCHI

The jumbo or king scallions are often 30–40 in (75 cm–1 meter) long, with a thick white root end. These jumbo scallions grow in Japan and Korea. If you cannot find king scallions, substitute medium-sized leeks. The flavor will be different, but the system of seasoning and assembly is the same. If leeks are used, the white root end is the most desirable. Trim off the green leaves and use them to cover the top of the seasoned chunks.

1 quantity rice porridge (page 41)
4 oz (115 g) fish paste
3 oz (85 g) chopped garlic
1 oz (30 g) chopped ginger
2 oz (60 g) red hot chili flakes
1 oz (30 g) red chili powder
5 oz (140 g) coarse sea salt
1 oz (30 g) sugar
6 lb (3 kg) king scallions or leeks, ends
    trimmed and cut into 1 ¹/₂ in (4 cm)
    lengths
1 radish, thinly sliced and julienned
3 oz (85 g) Indian mustard leaves, cut into
    1 ¹/₂ in (4 cm) lengths
1 carrot, thinly sliced and julienned

1. To make the seasoning, combine the rice porridge, fish paste, garlic, ginger, chili flakes and powder, salt, and sugar into a red paste.
2. Add the scallions or leek, radish, mustard leaves, and carrot. Toss gently to mix. Adjust the salt, sugar and chili if you desire a stronger flavor. Serve immediately as a spiced salad. Refrigerate the leftover part, allowing the kimchee to ferment slowly; this adds another taste dimension.

STUFFED WHOLE SQUID KIMCHEE
T'ONG OJINGO SOBAEGI

Cleaned squid is a convenient tube that can be filled and preserved. The texture of the squid with its hot filling makes for quite a spicy taste sensation.

5 lb (2.5 kg) medium-sized, fresh whole
    squid (about 8)
8 oz (230 g) coarse sea salt
$^2/_3$ cup crushed garlic
$^1/_4$ cup crushed fresh ginger
3 oz (85 g) red chili powder
2 oz (60 g) red hot chili flakes
$^2/_3$ cup fish sauce (fermented anchovy
    or shrimp extract)
2 radishes, thinly sliced and julienned
6 scallions, cut into 2 in (5 cm) lengths
$^1/_2$ cup Korean watercress (*minari*), cut into
    2 in (5 cm) lengths (optional)
$^1/_2$ large onion, thinly sliced (optional)
$^1/_3$ cup julienned carrot (optional)
$^1/_4$ cup chili threads (optional)

1. Clean the squid, discard the stomach and ink sac, and remove the skin. Sprinkle 3 oz (85 g) salt inside and outside the body. Cut off the tentacles and chop finely. Toss the chopped tentacles with 3 oz (85 g) salt in a separate bowl.
2. To make the stuffing, combine the garlic, ginger, chili powder and flakes, fish sauce and the remaining salt. Toss together the radish, scallions, and the *minari*, onion, carrot and chili thread, if used. Mix gently with the seasoning.
3. Drain the salted tentacles and mix well with the stuffing. Drain the squid body and stuff (not too tightly) with the prepared filling.
4. Pile the squid in a container, and cover with the remainder of the stuffing. Place a light weight on top of the mass and cover the lid. Ferment in a cool spot 2–3 weeks. To serve, slice the squid horizontally in $^1/_2$ in (1 cm) pieces.

WHOLE RADISH IN RICE BRAN KIMCHEE
MU SSALKYO CHORIM

This kimchee is considered a refreshing condiment, not a hot pickle. It is the rice bran (the coarse outer coat of the rice kernel after the rice is refined) that produces a mild, palatable flavor during fermentation. The preparation of the pickle is unconventional. The long, slender white radish is pulled from the sandy soil without mud clinging to it. Several of the radishes are tied together in a bundle and hung over a rope or bamboo pole in a shady or cool spot to dry for 2–3 days. The radishes wilt and become flexible enough to be twisted into a doughnut shape. Then they are ready to be fermented. This recipe is included here as an example of a traditional preparation.

5 long, slender radishes
2 lb (1 kg) rice bran
6 oz (170 g) coarse sea salt
2 oz (60 g) dried chili seeds

1. Partially dry the newly harvested slender radishes for 2–3 days in a shady area. Cut off almost all the leaves and stems and reserve.
2. Mix the rice bran evenly with 4 oz (115 g) salt and chili seeds.
3. Twist each radish into a doughnut shape and place it in a container. The radish should not be piled high but fitted in so that as much space as possible is used. Cover with the rice bran mixture so that all the space in filled. Top with the reserved stems and leaves (if any), and sprinkle over the remaining 2 oz (60 g) salt. Weight down with a heavy plate. This kimchee keeps for a long time and is fermented for 2–3 months in a cellar or cool area to avoid fluctuations in temperature. To serve, remove the radish from the container and rinse off the bran. Slice thinly and serve.

AUTUMN SOY BEAN LEAVES KIMCHEE
KAUL K'ONGNIP CHORIM

Mature, bright yellow autumn soy bean leaves are selected for freshness. If you cannot locate soy bean leaves, the recipe also works well with perilla or vine leaves. The leaves are eaten as a wrapper around cooked rice.

6 lb (3 kg) autumn soy bean leaves
2 gallons (10 liters) water, plus 2–3 cups extra
7 oz (200 g) coarse sea salt
1 quantity rice porridge (page 41)
4 oz (115 g) anchovy paste
3 oz (85 g) red hot chili flakes
3 oz (85 g) chopped garlic
2 oz (60 g) chopped ginger
8 oz (230 g) whole scallions, tied into bundles of 3–4

1. Tie the leaves together in bundles of 20–30 with string.
2. Prepare a brine with the water and 3 oz (85 g) salt. Rinse the leaf bundles briefly in the brine and drain.
3. To make the seasoning, combine the rice porridge, anchovy paste, chili, garlic, ginger, and 2 oz (60 g) salt. Hold the bundles by the tied ends and dip them firmly into the seasoning. Place them flat in a container. Cover with the bunches of scallions. Pour over 2 cups water and sprinkle with the remaining 2 oz (60 g) salt. Press down with a heavy plate. Cover, and ferment for 2–3 weeks or longer for long-term preservation.

RADISH STEMS WITH ANCHOVY PASTE KIMCHEE
MUCH'ONG CHOTKAL CHORIM

Whole stems and leaves of the radish are used in this kimchee, commonly served as a side dish. The scallions (spring onions) are also used whole.

5 lb (2.5 kg) radish stems and leaves
3 oz (85 g) coarse sea salt
1 quantity rice porridge (page 41)
6 oz (170 g) anchovy paste
3 oz (85 g) chopped garlic
1 oz (30 g) chopped ginger
5 oz (140 g) Chinese chives
2 oz (60 g) red hot chili flakes
3 oz (85 g) red chili powder
1/2 oz (15 g) sugar (optional)
2 lb (1 kg) scallions, root end trimmed, left whole

1. Toss the radish stems with salt and stand for 30 minutes.
2. To make the seasoning, combine the porridge, anchovy paste, chili flakes and powder, and sugar, if used. Drain the radish stems and reserve the liquid that has accumulated.
3. Toss together the radish stems, scallions and the seasoning. Put the mixture into a container. Rinse out the mixing bowl with the radish liquid and pour it over the kimchee. Cover and ferment for 2–3 days in summer, when the temperature is warm, and 1 week in autumn when the temperature is cooler. Refrigerate the kimchee after preparation.

WHOLE CUCUMBER IN RICE BRAN KIMCHEE
T'ONG OI SSALKYO CHORIM
(From previous page)

The young cucumbers are partially dried on a mat for 2–3 days to wilt them before pickling.

2 lb (1 kg) rice bran
6 oz (170 g) coarse sea salt
2 oz (60 g) dried chili seeds
5 lb (2.5 kg) cucumber, wilted

1. Mix together the rice bran, 4 oz (115 g) salt, and chili seeds.
2. Place the cucumbers neatly crossed in a container in a grid. The first layer is put down from back to front and filled in with the bran mixture. The next layer on top is placed left to right and covered with more bran. Repeat until you reach the top of the container. Sprinkle over with the remaining 2 oz (60 g) salt. Weight down the pickle with a heavy plate. Cover, and ferment for 2–3 months. To serve, remove the cucumbers, rinse off the bran, slice and serve.

FILLET OF FLOUNDER KIMCHEE
KAJAEMI SHIKHAE

This dish must be fermented for 3–4 weeks. It is a popular hot chili side dish.

7 oz (200 g) salt
3 lb (1.5 kg) small, firm-textured flounder fillet
3 oz (85 g) red chili powder
3 radishes, thinly sliced and cut into long juliennes
1 lb (500 g) cooked millet
3 oz (85 g) chopped garlic
2 oz (60 g) chopped ginger
4 oz (115 g) fish sauce
1 quantity rice porridge (page 41)
1 oz (30 g) red hot chili flakes
8 oz (230 g) scallions, halved lengthwise and cut into 3 in (7.5 cm) lengths

1. Rub 4 oz (115 g) salt into the fish fillets and allow to stand for 2 days in the refrigerator. The fish must be weighted down and covered. Cut into bite-sized pieces, 1 in x 2 in (2.5 cm x 5 cm). Rub with 3 oz (85 g) chili powder. Set aside.
2. Wilt the radish with 1 oz (30 g) salt, toss, and leave to stand.
3. To make the seasoning, combine the millet, garlic, ginger, fish sauce, rice porridge, chili flakes, and the remaining 2 oz (60 g) salt.
4. Mix this with the fish pieces, radish and scallions. Put into a container, cover, and allow to mature for 3–4 weeks. Serve as a side dish with a traditional Korean meal.

WHOLE RADDISH IN BRINE
TCHANJI MU

This pickle is prepared in late autumn and served in late spring before the arrival of summer crops. The whole radish is pickled in a simple but powerful brine with no herbs or spices that keeps the kimchee for a long time.

5 radish, desired size
1 quart (1–1.5 liters) water
1 cup coarse sea salt

1. Trim, clean, rinse, and drain the radish. Set aside overnight on a mat to slightly wilt. Fit the radishes tightly in a dry container. Weight them down with a heavy plate.
2. Combine the water and salt to make a brine. Pour over the radishes, making certain they are immersed in the liquid.
3. Keep the pickle in a dark, cool area. This pickle can be preserved for 4–6 months as long as the storage environment is well-maintained and is cool and clean. To serve, wash the radish in cold water to remove much of the salt. Then slice and serve, with a dash of vinegar and sugar mixture if desired.

GARLIC CLOVES PICKLE
AL MANUL CHORIM

Garlic is a powerful seasoning and can be made into a pickle for special occasions. It is renowned as an energy-producing pickle and for its robustness. The sweet-and-sour cloves are crunchy and served with beef, pork and chicken dishes. Some Korean households combine the garlic with the sweet, miniature green chili, which is less than 2 in (5 cm) long. Adjust the ratio of garlic to chili to taste.

5 lb (2.5 kg) fresh garlic cloves, peeled
1/2 cup sugar
4 oz (115 g) coarse sea salt
1 cup white vinegar
1 quart (1–1.5 liters) water

1. Rinse and drain the garlic cloves, and place neatly in a dry container. Add the sugar, salt, and vinegar. Fill the container with the water.
2. Weight down the garlic with a heavy plate, making certain the garlic does not float to the surface.
3. Cover, and keep the container in a cool and clean area and ferment for 6 months or more.

YEAR-ROUND KIMCHEE RECIPES

Think of the kimchee featured in this chapter as starter kimchee, if you like. They are short-term kimchee, and not meant for long-term storage or preservation. Most are ideal to serve as a salad with noodles, or as a nibbly with drinks, in the style of the Italian *antipasto*. The quantities of chili and chili powder are generous, so go easy at the start until you ascertain your chili heat tolerance.

PEARL ONION KIMCHEE
AL YANGP'A KKAKTUGI
(From previous page)

This variety of kimchee uses medium-sized pearl (pickling) onions.

6 lb (3 kg) whole pearl onions, peeled
5 oz (140 g) coarse sea salt
1 radish, thinly sliced and julienned
1 quantity rice porridge (page 41)
4 oz (115 g) fish sauce
3 oz (85 g) chopped garlic
1 oz (30 g) chopped ginger
1 oz (30 g) red hot chili flakes
2 oz (60 g) red chili powder
1 oz (30 g) sugar
4 oz (115 g) scallions, cut into 1 1/2 in (4 cm) strips
3 oz (85 g) carrots, thinly sliced and julienned

1. Toss the onions with 2 oz (60 g) salt. Set aside for 30 minutes.
2. To make the seasoning, combine the rice porridge, fish sauce, garlic, ginger, chili flakes and powder, 3 oz (85 g) salt and sugar, and mix well into a red paste. Toss together the paste, onions, scallions, and carrot. At this stage, adjust the salt, sugar, and chili to taste. If a more vivid flavor is wanted, add more seasoning. Put everything into a container and cover. Serve straight away as a fresh spiced salad. Refrigerate the balance to allow the kimchee to ferment slowly.

FIRM-HEADED CABBAGE JUICY KIMCHEE
YANG PAECH'U TONGCH'IMI

This is a cold, watery kimchee to be eaten with cold noodles. Serve it with the pickling broth.

1 large cabbage, cut into 2 in x 1/2 in (5 cm x 1 cm) lengths
8 oz (230 g) Korean watercress (minari), cut into 2 in (5 cm) lengths, stems only
4 oz (115 g) salt
3 oz (85 g) chopped garlic
2 oz (60 g) chopped ginger
3/4 quantity rice porridge (page 41)
1 oz (30 g) fresh red chili, seeded and cut into 2 in (5 cm) lengths
2 oz (60 g) chestnuts, boiled, peeled and thinly sliced (optional)
8 oz (230 g) scallions, halved lengthwise and cut into 2 in (5 cm) lengths
5 cups water

1. Mix the cabbage and minari and toss with 2 oz (60 g) salt. Put this into a container.
2. Add the garlic, ginger, rice porridge, red chili, chestnut, scallions, and the remaining 2 oz (60 g) salt. Pour the water over everything, cover and shake the container a few moments to distribute the flavors. Ferment lightly during the warm season for 2 days. Serve with any cold noodle dishes and snacks. Cold cooked rice is also dipped into the kimchee broth and eaten with the kimchee during summer days.

STUFFED FIRM-HEADED CABBAGE KIMCHEE
YANG PAECH'U MUL KIMCHI

These sausage-shaped rolls can be eaten freshly made or fermented for several days.

1 firm-headed medium-sized cabbage
6 oz (170 g) salt
2–4 cups water
3 radishes, thinly sliced and julienned
3 oz (85 g) chopped garlic
1 oz (30 g) chopped ginger
3 oz (85 g) fish sauce
1 oz (30 g) red hot chili flakes
1/2 oz (60 g) red chili powder
1 oz (30 g) sugar
6 oz (170 g) scallions, cut into thin strips
1/2 oz (60 g) red chili threads

1. Collect 35–40 medium-sized leaves from the cabbage. Remove the core of one or two cabbages after the large leaves are collected and pull off the small, curled leaves from the center. Julienne these small inner leaves finely. Sprinkle 1 tsp salt on the sliced inner leaves together with 1 cup water to make them wilt.
2. Prepare a brine with 3 oz (85 g) salt and water. Soak the larger outer leaves in the brine for 1–2 hours to wilt and soften. Drain.
3. Mix together the inner cabbage leaves and radish slices with 1 oz (30 g) salt. Reserve any liquid that accumulates.
4. To make the stuffing, combine the garlic, ginger, fish sauce, chili flakes and powder, and sugar. Add the cabbage and radish mixture to the stuffing, plus scallions and red chili threads. Set aside.
5. Rinse and drain the large wilted cabbage leaves. Put a leaf of cabbage on a flat surface. Add about 2 heaped tablespoons of the stuffing along the center rib of the leaf. Then roll it sideways from one side to another. Do not roll from the top to the bottom of the leaf. Repeat with the rest of the filling and cabbage.
6. Place all the stuffed rolls neatly into the container. Over the rolls, pour the liquid from the radish and add enough water to just cover them. Weight down the rolls with a plate or saucer. Lightly ferment the pickle for 2 days or serve immediately with a hint of vinegar.

COOL AND JUICY WHITE KIMCHEE
T'ONG PAECH'U PAEK KIMCHI

An all-season-style kimchee with a light, crunchy texture, this pickle may be compatible with most Asian and Western foods.

2 large Napa cabbages, about 4 lb (2 kg)
7 oz (200 g) coarse sea salt
1 gallon (5 liters) water
2 julienned radishes
2 cups scallions, cut into 1 1/2 in (4 cm) strips
1 medium-sized carrot, julienned
5 large cloves garlic, finely shredded
1/3 cup finely shredded fresh ginger
1 cup Korean watercress (*minari*), cut into 1 1/2 in (4 cm) lengths
4 chestnuts, boiled, peeled and shredded
3 Korean or Chinese dates, thinly shredded
1/2 Korean pear (*nashi*) or Beurre Bosc pear, peeled, sliced and julienned
1 tsp dried cloud's ear mushrooms, soaked in water until soft and shredded
1 tsp pine nuts
1 tsp sugar

1. Trim and discard the cabbage's outer leaves. Cut it in half lengthwise from the top down 1/3 of the length toward the root end. Hold both parts of the cabbage firmly and pull it in half. Repeat the process with the remaining cabbage.
2. To make the brine, dissolve 5 oz (140 g) salt in the water. Soak the cabbage halves in the brine for 16–18 hours or overnight. Cover the container with a saucer to completely immerse the vegetables. Drain and rinse under cold water. Drain again.
3. To make the stuffing, in a large enough mixing bowl, mix together gently the radish, scallions, carrot, garlic, ginger, watercress, chestnuts, dates, pear, mushrooms, pine nuts, sugar (if desired) and the rest of the salt (1 tablespoon). Toss gently.
4. Fill the cabbage leaves in layers with the stuffing. Take 2 of the outer leaves of each cabbage half and wrap around the cut side to hold everything together. Place in the pickling container. Cover, and sit for 2–3 days for fermentation in a cool spot. The kimchee ferments rapidly.

Note: 'Cloud's ear mushrooms' (*Auricularia polytricha*) are known as stone mushrooms in Korea. These grow on mountain rocks and stones, and are usually sold dried from Asian grocers. (They are sometimes available fresh.) The thin and small, black, crinkled pieces swell up to three times their size when soaked in cold water.

FRESH YOUNG SPINACH KIMCHEE
SHIGUMCH'I KOTCHORI

A dish characteristic of the Korean ability to use with thrift what nature has provided. Technically this is not a fermented pickle, but it comes under the kimchee category. It is one made of young spinach, including the roots.

6 lb (3 kg) fresh, tender, young spinach with
    roots attached
2 oz (60 g) chopped garlic
1 oz (30 g) chopped ginger
2 oz (60 g) red hot chili flakes
1 oz (30 g) red chili powder
2 oz (60 g) fish sauce
2 oz (60 g) salt
1 oz (30 g) sugar (optional)
1 radish, thinly sliced and julienned
1 onion, thinly sliced and julienned
4 oz (115 g) scallions, cut into
    2 in (5 cm) long strips
1 oz (30 g) red chili threads

1. Clean and trim the spinach thoroughly.
2. To make the seasoning, combine the garlic, ginger, chili flakes and powder, fish sauce, salt and sugar, if used.
3. Add the radish, onion, scallions, and spinach. Toss gently with the chili threads.
4. Place in a covered container if not eating immediately. If eating straight away, the kimchee can be served with a dash of vinegar and sesame oil.

CUT AND JUMBLED CABBAGE KIMCHEE
PAECH'U MAK KIMCHI

This is a popular daily kimchee. The vegetables are cut, seasoned, and tossed together. It can be eaten immediately as a salad or fermented for up to one week and served.

3 Napa cabbages, about 6 lb (3 kg)
1 radish
8 oz (230 g) coarse sea salt
1 gallon (5 liters) water
²/₃ cup fish sauce
1 quantity rice porridge (page 41) (optional)
¹/₃ cup red hot chili flakes
¹/₃ red chili powder
¹/₂ cup finely chopped garlic
¹/₃ cup finely chopped ginger
10 scallions, cut into 1 ¹/₂ in (4 cm) lengths

1. Remove 4–5 outer leaves from the cabbage and reserve. Cut the cabbage into 1 ¹/₂ in (4 cm) lengths. Thinly slice the radish and then cut into 1 in (2.5 cm) cubes.
2. To make the brine, dissolve 6 oz (170 g) salt in the water. Add the cabbage and leaves, the radish and soak for 4–5 hours. Drain, rinse in cold water and drain again.
3. To make the seasoning, put the fish sauce, porridge (if used), chili flakes and powder into a mixing bowl. Mix well, then add the garlic, ginger, scallions, cabbage, and radish. Toss the mixture gently to thoroughly mix. Firmly pack the mixture into a container. Cover with the reserved leaves and sprinkle in the remaining 2 oz (60 g) salt. Cover and ferment the mixture in a cool place for 2–3 days to allow the flavor to mature slightly. Or, serve the freshly tossed kimchee immediately with vinegar and sugar. If serving immediately, omit the rice porridge.

YOUNG GREEN SUMMER CABBAGE KIMCHEE
P'UT PAECH'U KOTCHORI

This recipe uses the leafy, lettuce-type summer cabbage that does not produce a head.

5 oz (140 g) salt
6 lb (3 kg) cabbage, whole leaves
3 oz (85 g) chopped garlic
2 oz (60 g) chopped ginger
4 oz (115 g) fish paste
1 oz (30 g) red hot chili flakes
2 oz (60 g) red chili powder
1 oz (30 g) sugar
8 oz (230 g) Korean watercress (minari)
8 oz (230 g) scallions, left whole
1 oz (30 g) sesame seeds, toasted
1 oz (30 g) chili threads
2 oz (60 g) white vinegar

1. Sprinkle 3 oz (85 g) salt over the cabbage leaves and toss well. Let stand for 1 hour to wilt. Rinse and drain.
2. To make the seasoning, combine the garlic, ginger, fish paste, chili flakes and powder, sugar and remaining 2 oz (60 g) salt. Add this to the cabbage, watercress, scallions, sesame seeds, chili threads, and vinegar. Toss well to mix. Serve as an instant kimchee (fresh salad).

WHOLE CARROT IN RICE BRAN PICKLE
TANGGUN SSALKYO CHORIM

You can combine the carrot prepared in this way with radish and cucumber to make a special dish. Arrange the white radish, green cucumber and orange carrot decoratively to make a tricolor side dish that is tasty and aesthetically pleasing.

2 lb (1 kg) rice bran
6 oz (170 g) coarse sea salt
2 oz (60 g) dried chili seeds
5 lb (2.5 kg) long tender carrots

1. Mix together the rice bran, 4 oz (115 g) salt, and the chili seeds.
2. Wilt and partially dry the carrots by tying several together in a bundle and hanging them over a rope or bamboo pole in a shady or cool spot for 2–3 days. The carrots become flexible enough to be twisted into a doughnut shape.
3. Twist each carrot into a doughnut shape and place it in a container firmly to take up as much space as possible. Alternate layers of carrot and rice bran (the bran should cover the spaces between the carrots so that all the space in the container is filled). Sprinkle over the remaining 2 oz (60 g) salt. Weight down the ingredients with a heavy plate. Cover, and ferment for 2–3 months. To serve, remove the carrots from the container and rinse off the bran. Slice thinly.

FRESH GINGER PICKLE
SAENGGANG CHORIM

This is more of a condiment than a pickle. Nevertheless, it is a common favorite. Serve as a refreshing condiment with steamed meat, chicken or raw fish dishes known as *Hoe*.

6 lb (3 kg) fresh ginger, peeled, and cut into 1/8 in (3 mm) slices
3 oz (85 g) salt
2 oz (60 g) sugar
3 cups water
1/2 tsp ascorbic acid (vitamin C), granules or powder
3 tsp white vinegar

1. Place the ginger slices in a clean, dry container. Add the salt, sugar, and mix well. Stand for 30 minutes to wilt.
2. Add the water, ascorbic acid, and vinegar to the container.
3. Cover and let the pickle ferment for 1–2 weeks in the fridge. This results in a fresh ginger flavor or a more intense pickle.

STUFFED CARROT KIMCHEE
TANGGUN SOBAEGI

Carrots were introduced into Korea only about 70–80 years ago. A carrot, according to old-time Koreans is an 'orange radish' because its firm texture is similar to that of a radish. This kimchee is a modern invention.

5 lb (2.5 kg) carrot, cut into chunks not more than 1 ¹/₂ in (4 cm) in diameter and 1 ¹/₂ in (4 cm) in length
5 oz (140 g) coarse sea salt
2 quantities rice porridge (page 41)
1 cup fish sauce
¹/₂ cup chopped garlic
¹/₃ cup chopped ginger
2 oz (60 g) red chili powder
1 radish, thinly sliced and julienned
4 scallions, cut into 1 ¹/₂ in (4 cm) pieces
2 oz (60 g) chestnut, boiled, peeled and julienned, or water chestnut, peeled and julienned
1–2 cups water

1. Scrub and peel the carrots. Make crossways slits about 1 ¹/₂ in (4 cm) deep into the stem end almost to the bottom. The carrot must remain whole. (Reserve the balance of the long, slender pieces of carrot for later.)
2. Sprinkle 3 oz (85 g) salt inside and outside the carrot chunks and let stand 2–3 hours. Then drain the liquid but do not rinse the chunks.
3. To make the stuffing, mix the rice porridge, fish sauce, garlic, ginger, chili, and the remaining 2 oz (60 g) of salt. Mix well, then add the radish, scallions, chestnut, and toss well with all the seasonings.
4. Stuff each carrot with about 1 tablespoon stuffing and place the carrots in an upright position in the container. Rinse out the mixing bowl with 1–2 cups water or just enough to cover the carrots. Ferment for 1–2 days and serve as a side dish with any food.

HOT AND SPICY CARROT CHUNKS
TANGGUN KKAKTUGI

According to some Korean cooks, a carrot is an orange radish. Use only fresh carrots for this kimchee.

6 lb (3 kg) fresh medium-sized carrots
5 oz (140 g) coarse sea salt
1 quantity rice porridge (page 41)
4 oz (115 g) fermented shrimp paste
3 oz (85 g) chopped garlic
1 oz (30 g) chopped ginger
2 oz (60 g) red chili powder
1 oz (30 g) sugar
1 radish, thinly sliced and julienned
4 oz (115 g) scallions, cut into 1 ¹/₂ in (4 cm) pieces
3 oz (85 g) chestnuts, boiled, peeled and julienned
1 oz (30 g) chili threads

1. Trim the carrots and cut into 1 in (2.5 cm) chunks. Toss with 3 oz (85 g) salt and set aside for 30 minutes. Drain and reserve the liquid that has accumulated.
2. To make the seasoning, combine the porridge, shrimp paste, garlic, ginger, chili powder, sugar, and 2 oz (60 g) salt into a red paste. Now add the radish, scallions, chestnut, and chili threads.
3. Add the carrot and its reserved liquid and toss gently to mix. Store in a container and ferment for 2 days. Serve as a side dish.

CUBED RADISH KIMCHEE WITH OYSTER
KKAKTUGI

A highly seasoned pickle with red chili-pepper, featuring cubed, crunchy radish. Reduce the quantities of chili to your liking.

7 medium-sized radishes
6 oz (170 g) coarse sea salt
2 quarts (2.5 liters) water
1 quantity rice porridge (page 41)
²/₃ cup fish sauce or fermented
    baby shrimp paste
¹/₄ cup red hot chili flakes
²/₃ cup red chili powder
¹/₃ cup finely chopped fresh ginger
²/₃ cup finely chopped garlic
¹/₄ cup sugar (optional)
10 scallions, cut into 1 ¹/₂ in (4 cm) lengths
1 cup fresh oysters, rinsed in a salt brine,
    then drained well

1. Trim off the leaves and root end of the radish. Reserve any leaves. Cut the radish into ³/₄–1 in (2–2.5 cm) cubes.
2. For the brine, dissolve 5 oz (140 g) salt in the water. Soak the radish in the brine for at least 3–4 hours. Cover the container with a saucer to completely immerse the radish. Drain and rinse under cold water. Drain again.
3. To make the seasoning paste, combine in a bowl the rice porridge, fish sauce or paste, chili flakes and powder, ginger, garlic and sugar, if used. Add the scallions and radish, and toss everything together gently. Put the mixture into a container, cover with the reserved leaves and sprinkle with 1 oz (30 g) salt. Cover and ferment for 3–4 days.

FIRM-HEADED CABBAGE KIMCHEE
YANG PAECH'U KOTCHORI

This is a different kind of kimchee in that the seasoning sauce can be prepared in advance and refrigerated until ready to use. The kimchee is not fermented but served immediately after preparation.

1/2 cup fresh red hot chili
1 medium-sized ripe red tomato
1 onion
4 oz (115 g) garlic
2 oz (60 g) ginger
2/3 cup rice porridge (page 41)
1 cup fish sauce
1 cup chopped scallions
1 tsp sugar
7 oz (200 g) coarse sea salt
2 large firm-headed cabbages, cut into
    1 in x 2 in (2.5 cm x 5 cm) pieces
1/2 cup white distilled vinegar

1. To make the sauce, coarsely blend together the chili, tomato, onion, garlic, ginger, rice porridge, fish sauce, 6 oz (170 g) salt, and sugar. Do not purée: the sauce must have some texture. (At this stage the sauce can be blanched and refrigerated for future use. It keeps, refrigerated, for up to 6 weeks.)
2. Toss the cabbage with the remaining salt and let stand for 30 minutes. Then gently press out the accumulated liquid.
3. Mix the cabbage, scallions and sauce, rinse out the processor with the vinegar and incorporate into the kimchee. Serve immediately as a fresh instant kimchee.

WRAPPED FIRM-HEADED CABBAGE KIMCHEE
YANG PAECH'U POSSAM KIMCHI

In this kimchee the chestnuts, pine nuts and the very thin, dry chili threads provide subtle flavor. Their inclusion is designed to 'gild the lily' and provide decoration.

3 medium-sized hard-headed cabbage
6 oz (170 g) coarse sea salt
4 cups water
2 quantities rice porridge (page 41)
3/4 cup fish sauce
2/3 cup garlic, chopped
1/4 cup ginger, chopped
1 oz (30 g) sugar
2 oz (60 g) red hot chili flakes
1 radish, julienned
2 cucumbers, cut into squares 1/8 in (3 mm)
    thick x 1 in (2.5 cm)
1 lb (500 g) carrot, thinly sliced and julienned
4 oz (115 g) scallions, cut into 1 1/2 in (4 cm)
    strips
2 oz (60 g) chestnuts, boiled, peeled, and
    julienned
1 oz (30 g) pine nuts
1/2 oz (60 g) dry chili threads
6 oz (170 g) fresh oysters rinsed in brine
    (optional)

1. Trim the root end of the cabbage. Remove and reserve 1/3 of the green outer leaves. Cut the remainder of the cabbage into 4 equal parts, then cut each part into 2 parts horizontally. Separate all the cut sections into loose leaves.
2. Prepare a brine with 3 oz (85 g) salt and 2 cups water. Soak the whole outer leaves and cut, loose ones in the brine for 2 hours to wilt them.
3. To make the seasoning, combine the rice porridge, fish sauce, garlic, ginger, 2 oz (60 g) salt, sugar, and chili flakes. Add the radish, cucumbers, carrot, scallions, chestnuts, pine nuts, chili threads, and oysters, if used. Toss the mixture together gently.
4. Drain all the cabbage leaves. Take 4 whole leaves and fit them into a Chinese-style soup bowl with the inner ends overlapping each other in 4 directions. This becomes the wrapper of the kimchee 'ball'.
5. The cut leaves of cabbage are mixed with the seasoning and other vegetables. Take 2 cups of this mixture and place it in the center of the cabbage leaf wrapper. The outer green parts of the leaves are folded over toward the center to shape a ball. Place in the container with the folded part up. Repeat with the rest of the cabbage and stuffing.
6. Rinse out the mixing bowl with 2 cups water and pour this into the container. Press down the container with a plate. Cover, and ferment for 1–2 days during warm weather or 3 days during cool temperatures. To serve, remove one or more wrapped balls to a serving plate and unfold.

INDEX